Sarah Saravanapavan .

# GERMAN VOCABULARY TOOLKIT

Published by Collins Educational
An imprint of HarperCollins*Publishers* Ltd
77–85 Fulham Palace Road
London
W6 8JB

www.**Collins**Education.com
On-line support for schools and colleges

10 9 8 7 6 5 4 3 2

ISBN 0-00-711466 4

British Library Cataloguing in Publication Data
A catalogue record for this book is available from the British Library.

Edited by Marieke O'Connor
Design and illustration by Pumpkin House
Cover design by Blue Pig Design Co
Production by Katie Morris
Printed and bound by Scotprint

# C O N T E N T S

## Welcome to the German Vocabulary Toolkit!

The aim of this book is to help you to learn the vocabulary which you will need to do well in the GCSE examination in German. The vocabulary listed in the book is based on the word lists in the specifications of the Assessment and Qualifications Alliance (AQA) and Oxford, Cambridge and RSA Examinations (OCR). Your teacher will tell you which examination board you are using.

You will not be allowed to use a dictionary in your examinations, so it is important that you have a good knowledge of vocabulary to back you up. The more words you know, the easier you will find it to do the questions well. Just as you can't build a house without bricks, you can't write in German without the words to put into the sentences.

## Structure of the book

This book is arranged to match the vocabulary topics of the specifications. The titles of these topics are given at the beginning of each section. In addition, each section uses colour to show the gender of the nouns. Masculine nouns ('der') are printed in blue; feminine nouns ('die') are printed in pink; neuter nouns ('das') are printed in orange. Plurals are printed in brown, verbs are printed in dark green, and adjectives are printed in light green. All other types of words are printed in purple. (There is some evidence to show that colour coding helps one remember which gender group a word belongs to by picturing the colour groups on the page.)

For each topic, vocabulary from the Higher Level is marked by an asterisk.

## The activities

After the list of words in each topic, there are a number of activities which will help you check whether you have learned the words. You should only do these activities when you have finished learning the vocabulary.

It would be possible to do the activities by writing the answers into the book, but it would be much better to write your answers onto a separate piece of paper. You could then do the activities several times – the more often you use paper. You could then do the activities several times – the more often you use the words the better they will become fixed in your memory. You will also be able to revise as the exam approaches.

Maybe you have bought the book a few weeks before the examination! In this case, do the exercises first. This will help you to find out which words you know and which ones you need to learn.

You will find the answers to the activities at the back of the book. Only look at the answers once you have done the exercises! Then you will find out which words you really have learnt. Don't look first! It won't help you to learn the words; it will only make you think that you know more than you really do.

You may have some answers which are different from the ones provided. This could well be the case. Don't automatically assume that you are wrong. Check with your teacher to see if your answer is also possible. (Maybe you could write to us at Collins and we could include your answers in a future edition!)

## Vocabulary learning

Vocabulary learning is an essential part of learning a foreign language and there are no short cuts. You have to build up your vocabulary by learning it slowly and gradually. Good linguists have a large vocabulary.

If you manage to learn ten words every day from Monday to Friday and use the weekend to revise them, you will learn fifty words a week. If you learn 50 words a week, you will learn 200 words in a month. 200 words every month means that you learn 2400 in a year. And 2400 words is more than enough for GCSE!

People learn vocabulary in different ways. You need to find the way which is best for you and use it regularly. In the next section we give you some tips on how to learn vocabulary. Try some of them out and you may find that learning vocabulary is more fun than you thought it was.

*Viel Spaß!*

# Tips on vocabulary learning

**1** Keep this book with you all the time. Use it when you have a spare moment. Every little helps! Test yourself regularly. Tick the words you really do know and concentrate on the ones you need to learn.

**2** Use this book often: when you are waiting for the bus; on the bus; when you have a few minutes to spare at home.

**3** Write out the words which you are finding difficult to learn. Write them slowly and carefully. Write them four or five times each.

**4** Keep a separate note book for words which you come across which are not in this book. Use this note book in the same way: go through it regularly, so that you learn these words too. The more words you know, the easier you will find it to do the tests in the examination.

**5** Make a set of vocabulary cards. Write the English word on one side of the card and the German word on the other. Go through the cards, testing yourself on the words. Put the words you know to one side. If you don't know a word, put it at the bottom of the pack, so that it comes up again until you really do know it.

**6** Get your parents, a relation or a friend to test you on the words you have to learn. It doesn't matter if they don't speak German. If they aren't sure if you got the word right, get them to ask you to spell it.

**7** Write down the words on little notes and put them around the house in places where you will see them regularly, e.g. by the television; in the bathroom; on the stairs; by the computer; by your bed; on the fridge. Tell your parents this is a vital part of your learning for GCSE!

**8** Use your vocabulary cards in the same way. Put one by the front door. Every time you come in or go out, look at the English word, say the foreign word, then turn the card over to see if you got it right. When you are sure you know the word, change the card for another one.

**9**     Say the words out loud when you are learning them. It helps you to remember them.

**10**    Make a cassette to help you learn the words. Write down a list of the English words and the German words. Speak the English words out loud one by one onto the cassette. After each English word, say the German word to yourself twice, without speaking out loud. This leaves a gap on the tape. When you have finished, play the tape and try to say the foreign word in the gap on the tape. When you can do this quickly for all the words, you will have learnt them. You can use the tape on your walkman.

**11**    If you are having difficulties remembering a word, ask a friend (or a teacher) to ask you what it is every time they pass you in the corridor in school. Make it into a kind of joke. You'll soon learn it then!

**12**    And don't forget to try and learn a small number of words each day. Remember: 10 a day = 50 a week = 200 a month = 2400 a year =

*Success at GCSE!*

## A note to parents

You can help your son or daughter by supporting them in their vocabulary learning. Even if you don't speak German, you can probably tell whether they know the word or not. If you are not sure, ask your son or daughter to spell it.

Allow your child to put some of the vocabulary learning tips into practice. It may mean having a lot of notes around your home and will make dusting difficult for a while - but you will be pleased when your child passes GCSE!

Take an interest in their vocabulary-learning and encourage them to do it. Try to have a regular time each day (e.g. after a meal) when you listen to the words they have learnt. Most children need a structure to help them learn. You can provide that.

|  |  |
|--------|---------|
| der Bart | beard |
| der Bruder | brother |
| der Cousin | cousin (male) |
| der Erwachsene | grown-up |
| der Familienangehörige | family member* |
| der Freund | friend |
| der Geburtstag | birthday |
| der Großvater | grandfather |
| der Hamster | hamster |
| der Herr | gentleman |
| der Hund | dog |
| der Junge | boy |
| der Körper | body |
| der Mann | man |
| der Nachbar | neighbour |
| der Name | name |
| der Onkel | uncle |
| der Opa/Opi | granddad |
| der Schnurrbart | moustache |
| der Schwager | brother-in-law* |
| der Sohn | son |
| der Vater | father |
| Vati | daddy |
| der Vetter | cousin (male) |
| der Vogel | bird |
| der Vorname | first name |
| der Wellensittich | budgerigar |
| der Wohnort | place of residence |
| der Zwilling | twin |

|  |  |
|--------|---------|
| die Brille | pair of glasses |
| die Dame | lady |
| die Familie | family |
| die Frau | woman |
| die Freundschaft | friendship* |
| die Geburt | birth* |
| die Glatze | bald head* |
| die Großmutter | grandmother |
| die Hausnummer | house number |
| die Katze | cat |
| die Kusine | cousin (female) |
| die Maus | mouse |
| die Mutter | mother |
| Mutti | mummy |
| die Nase | nose |
| die Oma | grandma |
| Omi | grandma |
| die Schwester | sister |
| die Staatsangehörigkeit | nationality* |
| die Tante | aunt |
| die Telefonnummer | telephone number |
| die Tochter | daughter |

|  |  |
|--------|---------|
| das Alter | age |
| das Auge | eye |
| das Baby | baby |
| das Einzelkind | only child |
| das Fräulein | young lady |
| das Haar | hair |

| das Haustier | pet |
| das Kaninchen | rabbit |
| das Kind | child |
| das Mädchen | girl |
| das Meerschweinchen | guinea pig |
| das Pferd | horse |
| das Taschengeld | pocket money |
| das Tier | animal |

| die Eltern | parents |
| die Geschwister | brothers and sisters |
| die Großeltern | grandparents |

*Plural*

| aussehen | to look (appearance) |
| beschreiben | to describe |
| buchstabieren | to spell |
| hassen | to hate |
| wohnen | to live |

*Verb*

| alt | old |
| blond | blond |
| dick | fat |
| dunkel | dark |
| geboren | born |
| geschieden | separated |
| getrennt | separated |
| groß | big, tall |
| hässlich | ugly |
| hell | light |

*adjectives*

| hübsch | pretty |
| jung | young |
| klein | small |
| kurz | short |
| lang | long |
| ledig | single* |
| mittelgroß | of medium height |
| schlank | slim |
| schön | beautiful |
| schwach | weak |
| stark | strong |
| Stief... | step... |
| tot | dead |
| verheiratet | married |

# Self, family and friends

**1** Which word is the odd one out? Also, in each group, write another word that <u>does</u> belong in the group.

**a** Hund    Katze    Meerschweinchen    Onkel    Pferd    _____

**b** Bruder    Haustier    Schwester    Mutter    Tante    _____

**c** getrennt    geschieden    ledig    hässlich    verheiratet    _____

**d** Tante    Brille    Bart    Auge    Schnurrbart    _____

**e** Oma    Mutter    Sohn    Kusine    Frau    _____

**2** Complete the table.

| Masculine | Feminine |
|---|---|
| Der Großvater | |
| | Die Schwester |
| Der Onkel | |
| Der Sohn | |
| | Die Kusine |

**3** Complete these star puzzles.

**a** Vater    M____    S_____

V_____ ◄ Familie ► T_____

O_____    K_____    G_____

**b** Katze    W_____    V_____

K_____ ◄ Haustier ► H_____

P_____    H_____    M_____

**4** Write in the consonants to complete these words.

**a** _ a a _

**b** _ _ e u _ _

**c** _ e _ u _ _ _ _ a _

**d** _ a _ _ _ e _ _ e _ _

**e** E _ _ a _ _ _ e _ e

**5** Write down the opposites.

alt       _____       schön       _____

dick       _____       lang       _____

schwach       _____       hell       _____

**6** Complete the family tree.

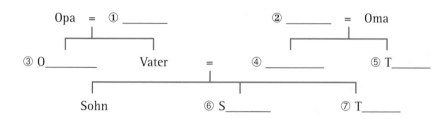

Opa = ① _____       ② _____ = Oma

③ O_____       Vater = ④ _____       ⑤ T_____

Sohn       ⑥ S_____       ⑦ T_____

**7** Put the words into the correct columns.

| Körper | Haustier | Familie |
|--------|----------|---------|
|        |          |         |
|        |          |         |
|        |          |         |
|        |          |         |
|        |          |         |

der Schnurrbart    der Vetter    das Kaninchen    die Glatze    das Auge
die Geschwister    der Hund    das Haar    die Nase
das Meerschweinchen    der Zwilling    die Katze    der Erwachsene
die Großeltern    der Wellensittich

**8** Solve the anagrams and give the English meaning.

legrotmißt     nerbistaeuchb     truGeb     Strrrnabuch     revtheraite

|  |  |  |  |
|---|---|---|---|
| der Bahnhof | railway station | die Brücke | bridge |
| der Blitz | lightning | die Burg | castle |
| der Dom | cathedral | die Fußgängerzone | pedestrian precinct |
| der Donner | thunder | die Gegend | area |
| der Einwohner | inhabitant | die Hitze | heat* |
| der Fluss | river | die Karte | map |
| der Frost | frost | die Kirche | church |
| der Fußgänger | pedestrian | die Kuh | cow |
| der Hafen | harbour | die Nähe | vicinity, neighbourhood |
| der Hügel | hill* | | |
| der Himmel | sky, heaven* | die Sonne | sun |
| der Jugendklub | youth club | die Stadt | town |
| der Markt | market | die Stadtmitte | town centre |
| der Marktplatz | market place | die Wettervorhersage | weather forecast |
| der Nebel | fog | | |
| der Ort | place | die Wolke | cloud |
| der Park | park | das Denkmal | statue |
| der Platz | square | das Dorf | village |
| der Regen | rain | das Einkaufszentrum | shopping centre |
| der Schauer | shower | | |
| der Schnee | snow | das Feld | field |
| der Sonnenschein | sunshine* | das Freibad | open-air swimming pool |
| der Spielplatz | play area | | |
| der Stadtrand | edge of town | | |
| der Sturm | wind storm | das Gewitter | storm |
| der Vorort | suburb | das Kino | cinema |
| der Wetterbericht | weather forecast | das Klima | climate |
| | | das Krankenhaus | hospital |
| der Wind | wind | das Land | land |
| der Zoo | zoo | das Museum | museum |
| | | das Rathaus | town hall |

| | | | |
|---|---|---|---|
| das Schaf | sheep | kalt | cold |
| das Schloss | castle | kühl | cool |
| das Schwimmbad | swimming pool | nass | wet |
| | | neblig | foggy |
| das Stadion | stadium | regnerisch | rainy |
| das Theater | theatre | sonnig | sunny |
| das Wetter | weather | stürmisch | stormy |
| das Zentrum | centre | trocken | dry |
| | | warm | warm |
| blitzen | there is lightning | windig | windy |
| | | wolkig | cloudy |
| donnern | to thunder | wolkenlos | cloudless* |
| frieren | to freeze | | |
| regnen | to rain | Grad | degrees |
| scheinen | to shine | Höchsttemperatur | highest temperature |
| schneien | to snow | | |
| | | Tiefsttemperatur | lowest temperature |
| bewölkt | overcast | | |
| feucht | damp* | | |
| heiß | hot | | |
| hitzefrei | school closed (hot weather) | | |

**1** What is the weather like? Write down the appropriate adjectives.

a      b      c      d      e      f      g      h

**2** Write down the names of these buildings. Don't forget the genders!

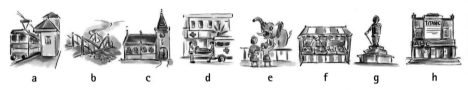

a      b      c      d      e      f      g      h

**3** What is in this picture? Write down the words.

**4** Put the words below into the correct columns.

| Stadt | Land | Wetter |
|---|---|---|
|  |  |  |
|  |  |  |
|  |  |  |
|  |  |  |
|  |  |  |

> das Dorf   der Schauer   der Dom   die Fußgängerzone   der Vorort
> neblig   das Gewitter   der Hügel   das Krankenhaus   der Fluss
> der Donner   das Theater   der Blitz   das Schaf   das Feld

**5** All these words have been split into two. Put the halves back together.

> Jugend   zentrum   platz   Sonnen   bericht   haus
> Spiel   klub   bad   Kranken   temperatur   schein
> Einkaufs   Schwimm   Höchst   Wetter

**6** Write down the opposites.

heiß   _____            regnerisch   _____

kühl   _____            bewölkt   _____

nass   _____

**7** Where might you see these signs?

a    **Nur für Fußgänger**        e    **Schwimmen: nur im Sommer**

b    **Nur für Kinder**        f    **Heute: *Hamlet***

c    **Tiere**        g    **Heute Abend: Disko**

d    **Fußballspiel heute**

**8** Complete the sentences.

a  Es gibt eine Brücke über dem _____.

b  Die Stadt hat fünfzigtausend _____.

c  Keine Schule heute: Wir haben _____.

d  Es gibt viele Kühe auf dem _____.

e  Wir wohnen nicht in der Stadtmitte, sondern in einem _____.

f  Es gibt einen guten Film im _____.

g  Im Winter haben wir immer viel _____.

h  Mein Haus ist in der _____ von dem Stadion.

| | | | |
|---|---|---|---|
| der Ausgang | exit | die Gesamtschule | comprehensive school |
| der Austausch | exchange | die Grundschule | primary school |
| der Bleistift | pencil | die Kantine | dining room |
| der Chor | choir | die Klasse | class |
| der Direktor | head teacher | die Klassenarbeit | class test |
| der Fehler | mistake | die Klassenfahrt | class visit |
| der Füller | fountain pen | die Mappe | folder |
| der Hof | yard | die Mittagspause | lunch break |
| der Kassettenrekorder | cassette recorder | die Naturwissenschaft | science |
| der Kindergarten | kindergarten | die Note | mark |
| der Klub | club | die Pause | break |
| der Kugelschreiber | biro | die Prüfung | exam |
| der Kuli | biro | die Realschule | secondary school |
| der Lehrer | teacher | die Regel | rule |
| der Ordner | file | die Schule | school |
| der Partner | partner | die Seite | page |
| der Radiergummi | rubber | die Strafarbeit | punishment |
| der Schuldirektor | head teacher | die Stunde | lesson |
| der Schüler | pupil | die Tafel | blackboard |
| der Schultag | school day | die Turnhalle | gym |
| der Stundenplan | timetable | die Umfrage | questionnaire |
| der Test | test | die Uniform | uniform |
| der Unterricht | lessons | | |

| | | | |
|---|---|---|---|
| die Antwort | answer | das Blatt | sheet of paper |
| die Aufgabe | exercise | das Buch | book |
| die Aula | assembly hall | das Fach | subject |
| die Band | band | das Gymnasium | grammar school |
| die Bibliothek | library | | |
| die Frage | question | das Heft | exercise book |

| | | | |
|---|---|---|---|
| das Internat | boarding school | korrigieren | to correct |
| das Klassenzimmer | classroom | lernen | to learn |
| das Labor | laboratory | malen | to paint |
| das Lineal | ruler | nachsitzen | to stay in |
| das Orchester | orchestra | schreiben | to write |
| das Papier | paper | singen | to sing |
| das Pflichtfach | compulsory subject | zeichnen | to draw |
| | | zuhören | to listen |
| das Semester | semester | | |
| das Wahlfach | optional subject | gemischt | mixed |
| | | leicht | easy |
| das Wörterbuch | dictionary | schwer | difficult |
| das Zeugnis | report | | |

ADJ

| | | | |
|---|---|---|---|
| die Ferien | holidays | Biologie | biology |
| die Hausaufgaben | homework | Chemie | chemistry |
| die Schularbeiten | school work | Deutsch | German |
| | | Drama | drama |
| abschreiben | to copy out | Englisch | English |
| anfangen | to begin | Erdkunde | geography |
| antworten | to answer | Französisch | French |
| aufhören | to stop* | Geschichte | history |
| beginnen | to begin | Informatik | information technology |
| dauern | to last | Kunst | art |
| enden | to finish | Mathematik | maths |
| erklären | to explain | Musik | music |
| fehlen | to be absent | Physik | physics |
| fertig sein | to be ready, finished | Religion | R.E. |
| | | Spanisch | Spanish |
| fragen | to ask | Turnen | P.E. |
| eine Frage stellen | to ask a question | Werken | C.D.T. |

**1** Sort these words into the right groups.

| Fächer | Sachen | Zimmer | Personen |
|--------|--------|--------|----------|
|        |        |        |          |
|        |        |        |          |
|        |        |        |          |
|        |        |        |          |
|        |        |        |          |
|        |        |        |          |

> Erdkunde   Schüler   Labor   Geschichte   Schuldirektor   Buch   Heft
> Kunst   Bleistift   Turnhalle   Aula   Lehrer   Werken   Ordner
> Informatik   Partner   Lineal   Turnen   Klassenzimmer   Bibliothek

**2** Write down the name of the subject.

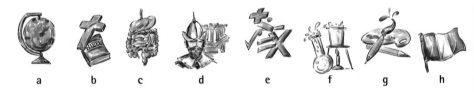

a        b        c        d        e        f        g        h

**3** Fill in the gaps in these sentences.

a  In meiner Schule gibt es mehr als tausend _____.

b  Die Naturwissenschaften, also _____, _____, und
   _____ sind meine Lieblingsfächer.

c  Im Moment gehe ich nicht zur Schule.  Wir haben sechs Wochen _____.

d  Ich kann heute Abend nicht ausgehen.  Ich muss die _____
   machen.

e  Mein Bruder ist sieben Jahre alt.  Er ist in der _____ .

f  In der Schule bekomme ich das Mittagessen in der _____.

g  Ich lerne Violine und in der Schule spiele ich im _____.

h  In Französisch schreibt der Lehrer die neuen Wörter an die _____.

**4** What is in the schoolbag?

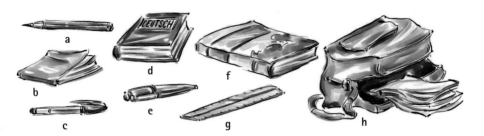

**5** Find the pairs in this list of words.

| | | | | |
|---|---|---|---|---|
| Informatik | das Labor | die Bibliothek | die Frage | das Wörterbuch |
| Mathematik | Musik | das Lineal | der Computer | Französisch |
| | die Antwort | das Buch | Chemie | der Chor |

**6** What word would be a definition for each sentence?

**a** Unsere Schule fährt nach Deutschland und dann kommen die deutschen Schüler zu uns.

**b** Hier kann ich sehen, was die nächste Stunde ist.

**c** In diesem Zimmer spielen wir Basketball, Tischtennis usw.

**d** Das ist für die Eltern am Ende des Schuljahres.

**e** Eine Gruppe von Schülern fährt in eine andere Stadt oder ein anderes Land.

**f** Die Arbeit, die man zu Hause machen muss.

**7** Find the two halves which go together to form a word.

| | | | | | |
|---|---|---|---|---|---|
| Kassetten | Kugel | Klassen | Stunden | Kinder | Wörter |
| | Schul | Mittags | Turn | Haus | |

| | | | | | | |
|---|---|---|---|---|---|---|
| halle | plan | aufgaben | direktor | schreiber | fahrt | rekorder |
| | | buch | garten | pause | | |

## Education

| | |
|---|---|
| der Arzt | doctor |
| der Beruf | job, career |
| der Erfolg | success* |
| der Handel | trade, commerce |
| der Ingenieur | engineer |
| der Lebenslauf | C.V.* |
| der Lehrling | apprentice |
| der Lohn | salary, wage |
| der Student | student |
| der Tierarzt | vet |
| der Tourismus | tourism |

| | |
|---|---|
| die Abschlussprüfung | leaving/final exam* |
| die Ausbildung | education, training |
| die Berufsausbildung | vocational training |
| die Disziplin | discipline |
| die Fachhochschule | college |
| die Hochschule | college, university |
| die Lehre | apprenticeship |
| die Leistung | achievement* |
| die Mittlere Reife | leaving exam (GCSE)* |
| die Oberstufe | upper school, sixth form |
| die Prüfung | test |
| die Uni | university |

| | |
|---|---|
| die Universität | university |
| die Zukunft | future |

| | |
|---|---|
| das Abitur | school leaving exam |
| das Gehalt | salary |
| das Resultat | result |
| das Studium | study |

| | |
|---|---|
| bestehen | to pass exam* |
| durchfallen | to fail exam* |
| heiraten | to marry* |
| studieren | to study |
| werden | to become |

| | |
|---|---|
| berufstätig | employed* |
| reich | rich |

# Work

| | |
|---|---|
| der Angestellte | employee |
| der Babysitter | babysitter |
| der Bäcker | baker |
| der Beamte | official |
| der Briefträger | postman |
| der Chef | boss |
| der Fleischer | butcher |
| der Kassierer | cashier |
| der Kaufmann | business man |
| der Krankenpfleger | male nurse |
| der Mechaniker | mechanic |
| der Metzger | butcher |
| der Polizist | policeman |
| der Teilzeitjob | part-time job |
| der Verkäufer | sales assistant |
| der Zahnarzt | dentist |

| | |
|---|---|
| die Arbeit | work |
| die Fabrik | factory |
| die Firma | firm |
| die Hausfrau | housewife |
| die Industrie | industry |
| die Krankenschwester | nurse |
| die Maschine | machine |
| die Nachricht | news, item of information |

| | |
|---|---|
| die Sekretärin | secretary |
| die Stelle | post, position, job |
| die Stewardess | stewardess |

| | |
|---|---|
| das Arbeitspraktikum | work experience |
| das Büro | office |
| das Marketing | marketing |
| das Stellenangebot | offer of a job, job advert |

| | |
|---|---|
| die Arbeitsstunden | working hours |

| | |
|---|---|
| arbeiten | to work |
| ausrichten | to give a message |
| austragen | to deliver (newspapers) |
| babysitten | to babysit |
| fotokopieren | to photocopy |
| liefern | to deliver |
| organisieren | to organise |
| sparen | to save |
| verdienen | to earn |
| zurückrufen | to phone back |

| | |
|---|---|
| am Apparat | on the telephone |
| arbeitslos | out of work |

## Education

**1** Put these words into chronological order.

> das Abitur     der Beruf     bestehen     die Oberstufe
> die Schule     das Stellenangebot     studieren

**2** Complete this star puzzle.

M _____     A _____     R _____

d _____     die Prüfung     b _____

s _____     E _____

**3** Complete the words by adding to the start letters. Give three words every time.

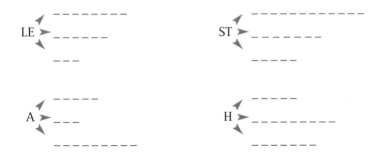

LE ► _ _ _ _ _ _ _
_ _ _ _ _ _
_ _ _

ST ► _ _ _ _ _ _ _ _ _ _
_ _ _ _ _ _ _
_ _ _ _ _

A ► _ _ _ _ _
_ _ _
_ _ _ _ _ _ _ _

H ► _ _ _ _ _
_ _ _ _ _ _ _ _ _
_ _ _ _ _ _

**4** Fill in the missing consonants in these words.

a   _ i e _ a _ _ _

b   _ u _ u _ _ _

c   _ e _ _ _ i _ _

d   I _ _ e _ i e u _

e   A u _ _ i _ _ u _ _

f   _ _ u _ i e _ e _

# Work

**1** Which job is suggested by these pictures?

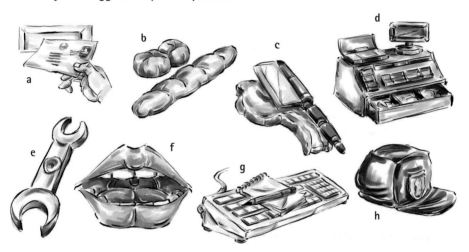

**2** What job is being described here?

a  Ich arbeite abends.

b  Ich repariere Autos.

c  Ich arbeite im Flugzeug.

d  Ich arbeite im Krankenhaus.

e  Ich arbeite bei der Post.

f  Ich arbeite im Supermarkt.

g  Ich arbeite zu Hause.

h  Ich arbeite im Büro.

**3** Write down:

a  three jobs beginning with K;

b  three places of work;

c  four jobs beginning with B.

**4** All these words have been split into two. Put the halves back together.

| | | | | | | | | |
|---|---|---|---|---|---|---|---|---|
| arbeits | Arbeits | Brief | foto | frau | Haus | job | Kauf | Kranken |
| los | pfleger | praktikum | mann | Teilzeit | träger | kopieren | | |

|  |  |
|---|---|
| der Ausstieg | exit (from bus/train) |
| der Bahnsteig | platform |
| der Bus | bus |
| der Busbahnhof | bus station |
| der D-Zug | express train |
| der Eilzug | stopping train |
| der Einstieg | entrance (to bus/train) |
| der Fahrer | driver |
| der Fahrkartenschalter | ticket office |
| der Fahrplan | timetable |
| der Fahrschein | ticket |
| der Flug | flight |
| der Flughafen | airport |
| der Führerschein | driving licence* |
| der Hauptbahnhof | main station |
| der Inter-City-Zug | intercity train |
| der Kofferraum | boot (of car)* |
| der Lastwagen | lorry |
| der Motor | engine |
| der Nahverkehrszug | local train |
| der Notausgang | emergency exit |
| der Parkplatz | car park, parking space |
| der Personenzug | slow train |
| der Reifen | tyre* |
| der Reifendruck | tyre pressure* |
| der Reisebus | coach |
| der Reisende | traveller |
| der Reisepass | passport |

|  |  |
|---|---|
| der Schaffner | guard, conductor |
| der Stau | traffic jam |
| der Verkehr | traffic |
| der Wagen | car |
| der Wartesaal | waiting room* |
| der Zug | train |
| der Zuschlag | supplement |
| die Abfahrt | departure |
| die Ankunft | arrival |
| die Ausfahrt | exit (from garage, etc.) |
| die Autobahn | motorway |
| die Bushaltestelle | bus stop |
| die Einfahrt | entrance (for vehicles) |
| die Fahrkarte | ticket |
| die Fahrt | journey |
| die Gepäckaufbewahrung | left luggage office |
| die Haltestelle | stop |
| die Hauptstadt | capital |
| die Hauptverkehrszeit | rush hour |
| die Heimfahrt | journey home* |
| die Linie | line, route |
| die Reifenpanne | flat tyre |
| die Rückfahrkarte | return ticket |
| die S-Bahn | suburban railway |
| die Station | underground station |

| die Straßenbahn | tram | fahren | to go (by vehicle) |
|---|---|---|---|
| die Tankstelle | petrol station | | |
| die U-Bahn | underground | fliegen | to fly |
| | | kommen | to come |
| das Abteil | compartment* | landen | to land (plane) |
| das Auto | car | parken | to park |
| das Autobahnkreuz | motorway junction* | reisen | to travel |
| | | starten | to take off (plane) |
| das Benzin | petrol | | |
| das Fahrrad | bicyle | überholen | to overtake* |
| das Flugzeug | plane | umsteigen | to change (train, etc.) |
| das Gepäck | luggage | | |
| das Gleis | track, platform | verpassen | to miss (train, bus) |
| das Mofa | moped | | |
| das Motorrad | motorbike | zurückkommen | to come back |
| das Öl | oil | | |
| das Parkhaus | multi-storey car park | bleifrei | leadfree |
| | | direkt | direct |
| das Rad | wheel, bike | einfach | single (ticket) |
| das Reiseziel | destination | früh | early |
| das Taxi | taxi | (zu) Fuß | on foot |
| | | hin und zurück | return (ticket) |
| abfahren | to depart | spät | late |
| anhalten | to stop | Überholverbot | no overtaking |
| ankommen | to arrive | Verspätung haben | to be late |
| aussteigen | to get off | | |
| bremsen | to brake* | | |
| einsteigen | to get on | | |
| entwerten | to validate (ticket) | | |
| erreichen | to reach | | |

**1** Jigsaw words. **Make up eight words from these parts of words. Each word has three parts.**

> Auto bahn bahn bahn Bus Bus City fahr halte Haupt Haupt hof hof
> Inter karte kreuz Nah Rück stelle verkehrs verkehrs zeit Zug zug

**2** Put the words into the correct column.

| Auto | Zug | Flugzeug |
|---|---|---|
|  |  |  |
|  |  |  |
|  |  |  |
|  |  |  |
|  |  |  |

> der Bahnsteig    die Einfahrt    fliegen    der Flug    der Flughafen
> der Hauptbahnhof    der Kofferraum    landen    der Schaffner    starten
> der Stau    die Tankstelle    überholen    der Wartesaal    der Zuschlag

**3** Label these pictures.

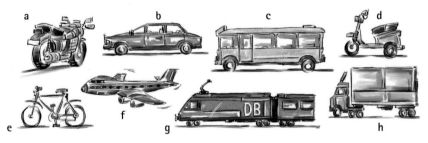

a    b    c    d

e    f    g    h

**4** Put these verbs in the order that they would occur if you were on a journey.

> abfahren    anhalten    ankommen    aussteigen
> einsteigen    fahren    überholen    zurückkommen

**5** Write down:

   **a** two words ending with 'stelle'

   **b** three words ending with 'bahn'

   **c** four words ending with 'fahrt'

**6** Add a part to the front of these words to make another word.

   **a** Ausgang    **b** Wagen    **c** Fahrkarte    **d** Bahnhof    **e** Zug
   **f** Rad    **g** Bus    **h** Hafen

**7** Fill in the gaps in these sentences.

   **a** Der Zug hat fünf Minuten _____ .

   **b** Der Zug kommt in zwanzig Minuten. Wir können in dem
      _____ sitzen.

   **c** Ich bin 17 Jahre alt. Ich darf einen _____ haben.

   **d** Das Gepäck ist in dem _____ von dem Auto.

   **e** Ich fahre nicht sehr oft in die Stadt. Ich kann nie einen
      _____ finden.

   **f** Die Autos stehen auf der Autobahn. Es gibt einen _____ .

   **g** Wir fliegen um 4 Uhr. Wir müssen um 2 Uhr am _____ sein.

   **h** Ich fahre nicht gern. Ich gehe lieber _____ _____ .

**8** Complete the words by adding to the letters given. Give three words every time.

REI ➤
   – – –
   – – – – – –
   – – – – –

FAHR ➤
   – – –
   – – – –
   – – – – –

ST ➤
   – – – – –
   – – – – – – – –
   – –

FL ➤
   – –
   – – – –
   – – – – – –

| | | | |
|---|---|---|---|
| der Ausflug | excursion | die Eissporthalle | ice rink* |
| der Badeanzug | swimming costume | die Fähre | ferry |
| | | die Führung | conducted tour* |
| der Balkon | balcony | die Gastfamilie | host family |
| der Berg | mountain | die Gastfreundschaft | hospitality |
| der Blick | view | die Grenze | border, frontier* |
| der Freizeitpark | theme park* | die Information | information |
| der Fremde | stranger | die Insel | island* |
| der Gast | guest | die Küste | coast |
| der Koffer | suitcase | die Landschaft | scenery |
| der Prospekt | brochure | die Reise | journey |
| der Reiseführer | guide book* | die Rundfahrt | tour |
| der Reiseleiter | tour leader* | die See | sea |
| der Rucksack | rucksack | die Sehenswürdigkeit | sight |
| der Ruhetag | closing day | | |
| der Sand | sand | die Sonnenbrille | sun glasses |
| der See | lake | die Sonnencreme | sun cream |
| der Stadtbummel | walk round town | die Stadtrundfahrt | tour of town |
| | | die Terrasse | terrace |
| der Strand | beach | die Tour | tour |
| der Tierpark | zoo* | die Touristeninformation | tourist information |
| der Tourist | tourist | | |
| der Turm | tower* | die Überfahrt | (sea) crossing |
| der Urlaub | holiday, vacation | die Unterschrift | signature |
| | | die Versicherung | insurance* |
| der Zoll | customs* | die Zollkontrolle | customs* |
| der Zollbeamte | customs official* | | |

| | |
|---|---|
| das Boot | boat |
| das Gebiet | area |
| das Gebirge | mountains* |
| das Informationsbüro | information office |

| | |
|---|---|
| die Aussicht | view |
| die Badehose | swimming trunks |
| die Broschüre | brochure |

| | |
|---|---|
| das Land | country |
| das Meer | sea |
| das Reisebüro | travel agent's |
| das Schiff | ship |
| das Souvenir | souvenir |
| das Trinkgeld | tip |
| das Verkehrsamt | tourist office |

| | |
|---|---|
| die Ferien | holidays |

| | |
|---|---|
| beilegen | to enclose* |
| besichtigen | to view, sightsee |
| buchen | to book |
| bummeln | to stroll* |
| lösen | to buy (a ticket) |
| mieten | to hire, rent* |
| packen | to pack |
| planen | to plan |
| reservieren | to reserve |
| rudern | to row* |
| (sich) sonnen | to sunbathe |
| unterschreiben | to sign |

| | |
|---|---|
| seekrank | sea sick |
| sehenswert | worth seeing |
| zollfrei | duty free |

## 1 Find synonyms for the following words.

**a** die Tour _____    **d** reservieren _____

**b** die Broschüre _____    **e** das Informationsbüro _____

**c** die See _____    **f** die Ferien _____

## 2 Put the words into the correct columns.

| Landschaft | Tour | Personen |
|---|---|---|
|  |  |  |
|  |  |  |
|  |  |  |
|  |  |  |
|  |  |  |

der Berg   besichtigen   der Fremde   der Gast   die Insel   die Küste
der Reiseführer   der Reiseleiter   der See   die Sehenswürdigkeit
die Stadtrundfahrt   der Strand   der Tourist   der Turm   der Zollbeamte

## 3 Fill in the missing words on this postcard.

Schöne Grüße aus dem Urlaub!

Der (a)_____ aus dem Hotelfenster ist sehr schön. Das Wetter ist auch sehr schön: Wir sitzen jeden Tag am (b)_____ und (c)_____ _____ . Es ist gut, dass ich meine (d)_____ und (e)_____ mitgebracht habe. Abends sitzen wir auf dem (f)_____.

Wir haben viele (g)_____ gemacht und der (h)_____ hat viele Information gegeben.

Ich habe den Urlaub im Reisebüro (i)_____ und ich habe einen (j)_____ vom Verkehrsamt bekommen.

**1** **Match the correct halves of these sentences.**

**a** Die Überfahrt war sehr stürmisch

**b** Der Blick aus dem Fenster ist schön:

**c** Wir haben einen Stadtbummel gemacht

**d** Italien ist ein schönes Land:

**e** Ich habe in dem Reiseführer gelesen,

**1** Es hat viele Sehenswürdigkeiten.

**2** dass der Turm in der Stadtmitte sehenswert ist.

**3** und ich habe viele Souvenirs gekauft.

**4** und ich war seekrank.

**5** Wir können das Meer sehen.

**2** **Label this picture.**

| der Aufzug | lift |
|---|---|
| der Balkon | balcony |
| der Campingplatz | camp site |
| der Eingang | entrance |
| der Empfang | reception |
| der Fahrstuhl | lift |
| der Fernseher | TV set |
| der Gang | corridor |
| der Gast | guest |
| der Lift | lift |
| der Rasierapparat | electric shaver |
| der Schlafsack | sleeping bag |
| der Schlüssel | key |
| der Speisesaal | dining room |
| der Waschraum | wash room |
| der Zeltplatz | camp site |

| die Abreise | departure |
|---|---|
| die Anmeldung | reception |
| die Dusche | shower |
| die Halbpension | half board |
| die Jugendherberge | youth hostel |
| die Mehrwertsteuer | value added tax |
| die Nacht | night |
| die Pension | boarding house |
| die Rechnung | bill |
| die Reservierung | reservation |
| die Seife | soap |
| die Übernachtung | overnight stay |
| die Unterkunft | board |
| die Vollpension | full board |

| die Zahnbürste | tooth brush |
|---|---|
| die Zahnpasta | tooth paste |

| das Badetuch | bath towel |
|---|---|
| das Bauernhaus | farm house |
| das Doppelzimmer | double room |
| das Einzelzimmer | single room |
| das Familienzimmer | family room |
| das Frühstück | breakfast |
| das Gasthaus | pub |
| das Handtuch | hand towel |
| das Hotel | hotel |
| das Waschbecken | wash basin |
| das WC | toilet, WC |
| das Zelt | tent |
| das Zimmer | room |

| bestätigen | to confirm |
|---|---|
| bleiben | to stay |
| buchen | to book |
| reservieren | to reserve |
| übernachten | to stay overnight |
| zelten | to camp |

| besetzt | occupied, full |
|---|---|
| frei | free |
| Fremdenzimmer | rooms to let* |
| inbegriffen | included |
| inklusive | inclusive |

**1** Write down the names of these items.

a    b        c      d      e        f   g      h

**2** With what do you connect these words? Write C for the campsite, H for the hotel and B for both.

a  der Fahrstuhl    **b**  der Schlafsack    **c**  die Dusche    **d**  Halbpension
**e**  der Schlüssel    **f**  der Empfang    **g**  die Übernachtung    **h**  das Zelt
**i**  das Doppelzimmer    **j**  der Waschraum    **k**  der Speisesaal

**3** **a**  Write down three words for 'lift'.
   **b**  Write down four words ending with –zimmer.

**4** These words have all been split into two. Match up the two halves.

| apparat    becken    Fahr    Hand    herberge    Jugend    kunft    pension |
|---|
| platz    Rasier    stuhl    tuch    Unter    Voll    Wasch    Zelt |

**5** Complete these words by adding to the letters given. Give three words every time.

S &gt; _ _ _ _ _ _ _ _ _
    _ _ _ _ _ _ _ _
    _ _ _ _

R &gt; _ _ _ _ _ _
    _ _ _ _ _ _ _ _ _ _
    _ _ _ _ _ _ _ _ _ _

**6** Correct the following sentences.

  **a**  Wir zelten in der Jugendherberge.

  **b**  Wir bekommen Vollpension: Frühstück und Abendessen.

  **c**  Wir essen in dem Aufzug im Hotel.

  **d**  Mein Bruder und ich schlafen in einem Einzelzimmer.

| | | | |
|---|---|---|---|
| der Amerikaner | American | die Französin | Frenchwoman |
| der Brieffreund | pen friend | die Niederlande | Netherlands |
| der Belgier | Belgian | die Nordsee | North Sea |
| der Däne | Dane | die Ostsee | Baltic Sea |
| der Deutsche | German | die Person | person |
| der Engländer | Englishman | die Schweiz | Switzerland |
| der Franzose | Frenchman | die Türkei | Turkey |
| der Fremde | foreigner | | |
| der Grieche | Greek | das Ausland | foreign countries |
| der Holländer | Dutchman | | |
| der Irländer | Irishman | das Mittelmeer | Mediterranean |
| der Italiener | Italian | | |
| der Kanal | English Channel | die Alpen | the Alps |
| der Norden | north | die Leute | people |
| der Norweger | Norwegian | die USA | USA |
| der Osten | east | | |
| der Österreicher | Austrian | Afrika | Africa |
| der Pole | Pole | Amerika | America |
| der Portugiese | Portugese | Bayern | Bavaria |
| der Rhein | River Rhine | Belgien | Belgium |
| der Russe | Russian | Dänemark | Denmark |
| der Schotte | Scot | Deutschland | Germany |
| der Schweizer | Swiss | England | England |
| der Spanier | Spaniard | Europa | Europe |
| der Süden | south | Frankreich | France |
| der Türke | Turk | Griechenland | Greece |
| der Westen | west | Großbritannien | Great Britain |
| | | Irland | Ireland |
| die Donau | River Danube | Italien | Italy |
| die Engländerin | Englishwoman | Köln | Cologne |
| die EU | European Union | München | Munich |

| | | | |
|---|---|---|---|
| Norwegen | Norway | schwedisch | Swedish |
| Österreich | Austria | schweizerisch | Swiss |
| Polen | Poland | spanisch | Spanish |
| Russland | Russia | türkisch | Turkish |
| Schottland | Scotland | walisisch | Welsh |
| Schweden | Sweden | | |
| Spanien | Spain | | |
| Wales | Wales | | |
| Wien | Vienna | | |

| | |
|---|---|
| im Ausland | abroad |
| ins Ausland fahren | to go abroad |

| | |
|---|---|
| amerikanisch | American |
| belgisch | Belgian |
| britisch | British |
| dänisch | Danish |
| deutsch | German |
| englisch | English |
| französisch | French |
| fremd | foreign |
| griechisch | Greek |
| holländisch | Dutch |
| irisch | Irish |
| italienisch | Italian |
| norwegisch | Norwegian |
| österreichisch | Austrian |
| polnisch | Polish |
| portugiesisch | Portugese |
| russisch | Russian |
| schottisch | Scottish |

**1** Where are these capital cities?  Write down the country.

a London      d Washington      g Edinburgh      i Madrid
b Paris       e Rom             h Wien           j Berlin
c Athen       f Brüssel

**2** Complete the table.

| England | englisch | |
| | deutsch | |
| Frankreich | | |
| Italien | | der Italiener |
| | griechisch | |
| | | der Spanier |
| | | der Türke |
| | | der Schweizer |

**3** Which language is this? Write it down in German.

a Good morning!      c Guten Tag!      e Buenos dias!      g Lyi  günler!
b Bonjour!           d Buongiorno!     f Kalimera!         h Bom dia!

**4** Label this map.

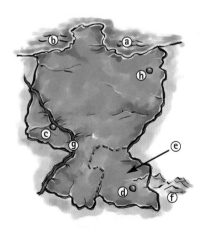

**5 Wie heißt/heißen. . .**

**a** das Meer zwischen Deutschland und Skandinavien?

**b** die See zwischen Deutschland und England?

**c** das Wasser zwischen Belgien/Frankreich und England?

**d** die Hauptstadt von Österreich?

**e** das Meer zwischen Europa und Afrika?

**f** ein Land in Europa mit vier Sprachen?

**g** die Berge in Süddeutschland und Österreich?

**6 Which countries do cars with these registration plates come from?**

**7 In which country can you see the following sights?**

    a          b               c              d         e

**8 Solve the anagrams.**

    **a** denfreiBurf        **e** Banery

    **b** ide aonuD          **f** zarFnose

    **c** cheatislini        **g** sad retiMeeltm

    **d** edi Ndreose       **h** opErau

## Services

| | |
|---|---|
| der Anruf | telephone call |
| der Anrufbeantworter | answering machine* |
| der Brief | letter |
| der Briefkasten | letter box |
| der Euro | Euro |
| der Euroschein | Euro note* |
| der Geldwechsel | bureau de change |
| der Hörer | telephone receiver |
| der Kurs | exchange rate |
| der Reisescheck | traveller's cheque |

| | |
|---|---|
| die Ansichtskarte | picture postcard |
| die Bank | bank |
| die Briefmarke | stamp |
| die E-Mail | e-mail |
| die Münze | coin |
| die Post | post office |
| die Postkarte | post card |
| die Postleitzahl | post code |
| die Sparkasse | bank |
| die Telefonkarte | phone card |
| die Telefonnummer | telephone number |
| die Telefonzelle | telephone box |
| die Vorwahlnummer | dialling code |
| die Wechselstube | bureau de change |

| | |
|---|---|
| das Fax | fax |
| das Fundbüro | lost property office* |
| das Geld | money |
| das Kleingeld | small change |
| das Postamt | post office |
| das Schließfach | locker* |

| | |
|---|---|
| abschicken | to send off |
| anrufen | to telephone |
| einwerfen | to put money in |
| faxen | to fax* |
| mailen | to send an e-mail* |
| mieten | to rent, hire |
| schicken | to send |
| telefonieren | to telephone |
| verbinden | to connect |
| wählen | to dial |
| wechseln | to change |

| | |
|---|---|
| besetzt | engaged (phone) |

## Finding the Way

| | |
|---|---|
| der Kilometer | kilometre |
| der Meter | metre |
| der Parkschein | parking ticket* |
| der Stadtplan | town plan |
| der Wegweiser | signpost |

| | |
|---|---|
| die Adresse | address |
| die Ampel | traffic lights |
| die Ecke | corner |
| die Einbahnstraße | one way street |
| die Hauptstraße | main street |
| die Kreuzung | crossroads |
| die Landkarte | map |
| die Meile | mile |
| die Richtung | direction |
| die Seite | side |
| die Straße | street |
| die Tiefgarage | underground car park* |

| | |
|---|---|
| das Ende | end |
| das Parkhaus | multi-storey car park* |
| das Schild | sign |

| | |
|---|---|
| finden | to find |
| folgen | to follow |
| gehen | to go |
| lösen | to buy (ticket)* |
| nehmen | to take |

| | |
|---|---|
| suchen | to look for |
| überqueren | to cross |

| | |
|---|---|
| dritte | third |
| drüben | over there |
| entlang | along |
| erste | first |
| gegenüber | opposite |
| geradeaus | straight on |
| hinauf | up |
| hinunter | down |
| letzt | last |
| links | left |
| mindestens | at least |
| nächst | next |
| rechts | right |
| um | around |
| ungefähr | approximately |
| weit | far |
| zweite | second |

| | |
|---|---|
| auf der linken / rechten Seite | on the left- / right-hand side |
| Entschuldigen Sie | Excuse me |
| Entschuldigung! | Excuse me! |
| Wie komme ich am besten zum / zur | Where is / how do I get to |
| wo | where |

## Services

### 1 Label the letter.

b_____

d_____

f_____

g_____

a_____

c_____

e_____

h_____

### 2 Write the German words for the following:

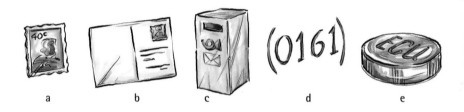

a      b      c      d      e

### 3 Match the verb with the appropriate noun.

  **a** der Kurs      **b** der Brief      **c** die E-Mail      **d** die Telefonzelle

   wählen        mailen        schicken        wechseln

### 4 Put these phrases into the correct order. What activity are you doing here?

verbinden      sprechen      Auf Wiederhören sagen      den Hörer auflegen
Geld einwerfen      wählen      den Hörer abnehmen

### 5 Fill in the gaps in these sentences.

  **a** Ich habe meinem Freund einen _____ geschrieben.

  **b** Er hat auch einen Computer. Ich kann eine E-Mail _____.

  **c** Im Urlaub habe ich meinen Freunden eine _____ geschickt.

  **d** Ich muss telefonieren. Ist hier in der Nähe eine _____?

  **e** Ich kann ohne Geld telefonieren. Ich habe eine _____.

# Finding the Way

**1** Write down the correct German word.

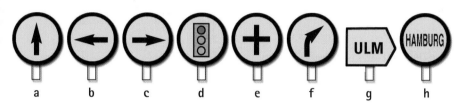

a     b     c     d     e     f     g     h

**2** Write down the opposites.

**a** hinauf   _____      **c** erste     _____

**b** links   _____      **d** suchen   _____

**3** Fill in the missing words in this conversation.

a)_____! Ich b)_____ die Post. c)_____ ist sie, bitte? Ich kann sie auf dem d)_____ nicht e)_____.

Die Post? Ja, f)_____ Sie hier g)_____. h)_____ Sie die i)_____ Straße j)_____ . Die Post ist auf der k)_____ Seite. Es ist l)_____ ein Kilometer von hier entfernt.

> erste    finden    gehen    geradeaus    Entschuldigung!    links
> nehmen    rechten    Stadtplan    suche    ungefähr    wo

**4** Solve the anagrams.

**a** grunzKeu            **e** edgaresau

**b** tanSltapd           **f** kanteaLdr

**c** nequrrbeeu         **g** guntRihc

**d** brasthEneißan

| | | | |
|---|---|---|---|
| der Abschleppdienst | tow-away service* | die Erste Hilfe | first aid |
| der Arm | arm | die Feuerwehr | fire brigade* |
| der Arzt | doctor | die Gefahr | danger |
| der Bauch | stomach | die Gesundheit | health |
| der Daumen | thumb* | die Grippe | flu |
| der Durchfall | diarrhoea | die Hand | hand |
| der Erste-Hilfe-Kasten | first aid box | die Hilfe | help |
| der Finger | finger | die Krankheit | illness |
| der Fuß | foot | die Lippe | lip |
| der Hals | neck | die Medizin | medicine |
| der Kopf | head | die Panne | breakdown* |
| der Körper | body | die Pastille | pastille |
| der Krankenwagen | ambulance | die Polizei | police |
| der Krebs | cancer | die Polizeiwache | police station* |
| der Magen | stomach | die Reparaturwerkstatt | garage (repair)* |
| der Mund | mouth | die Reifenpanne | puncture* |
| der Notruf | emergency call | die Rettung | rescue |
| der Rücken | back | die Salbe | cream (to rub on)* |
| der Schnupfen | cold | die Schulter | shoulder |
| der Sicherheitsgurt | safety belt | die Sicherheit | safety |
| der Sonnenbrand | sun burn | die Sprechstunde | surgery, consulting hours |
| der Termin | appointment* | die Stimme | voice |
| der Unfall | accident | die Tablette | tablet |
| der Zahn | tooth | die Temperatur | temperature |
| der Zeuge | witness* | die Wunde | wound* |
| der Zusammenstoß | car crash* | die Zunge | tongue* |

| | |
|---|---|
| die Brust | chest, breast |
| die Erkältung | cold |

| | | | |
|---|---|---|---|
| das Bein | leg | blass | pale |
| das Blut | blood* | gebrochen | broken |
| das Fieber | fever | gefährlich | dangerous |
| das Gesicht | face | gesund | healthy |
| das Heftpflaster | sticking plaster | kaputt | broken |
| das Knie | knee | krank | ill |
| das Medikament | medicine | verboten | forbidden |
| das Ohr | ear | verletzt | wounded |
| | | verstopft | constipated* |
| die Nerven | nerves | | |
| die Schmerzen | pains | Achtung! | Watch out! |
| | | Gesundheit! | Bless you! |
| aufpassen | to pay attention | mir ist übel | I feel sick |
| | | Vorsicht! | Watch out! |
| (sich) beschweren | to complain* | Was ist los? | What's the matter? |
| brechen | to break | | |
| bremsen | to brake* | Kopfschmerzen | headache |
| drücken | to press | Magenschmerzen | stomach ache |
| (sich) erbrechen | to be sick | Ohrenschmerzen | earache |
| (sich) erkälten | to catch cold | Zahnschmerzen | tooth ache |
| fallen | to fall | | |
| (sich) fühlen | to feel | | |
| geschehen | to happen | | |
| helfen | to help | | |
| husten | to cough* | | |
| leiden | to suffer* | | |
| niesen | to sneeze* | | |
| reparieren | to repair | | |
| stehlen | to steal* | | |
| untersuchen | to examine* | | |
| versichern | to insure* | | |
| weh tun | to hurt | | |

**1** Label the parts of the body indicated.

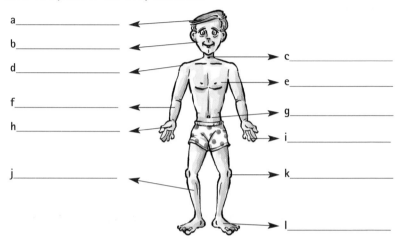

a_____

b_____

d_____

                                 c_____

                                 e_____

f_____

h_____

                                 g_____

                                 i_____

j_____

                                 k_____

                                 l_____

**2** Label the parts of the head indicated.

a_____

                                 c_____

b_____

                                   d_____

e_____ (Unit 1)

                                 f_____

g_____

                                 h_____

**3** Is the person ill (krank)? If so write K. Are they injured (verletzt)? Then write V. Or is it something dangerous (gefährlich)? Write G.

a  Ich fahre ohne Sicherheitsgurt.

b  Ich habe mein Bein gebrochen.

c  Ich muss ein Medikament nehmen.

d  Ich habe ein Heftpflaster auf dem Knie.

e  Ich nehme zu viele Tabletten.

f  Vorsicht! Hier kannst du fallen.

**g** Ich huste und ich habe mich erkältet.

**h** Mein Arm tut weh.

**i** Du fährst zu schnell. Es kann einen Unfall geben.

**4 Find the odd one out.**

**a** Knie    Bein    Fuß    Hand    Fieber

**b** verletzt    verboten    verstopft    kaputt    krank

**c** Krebs    Grippe    Tablette    Schnupfen    Erkältung

**d** blass    krank    husten    gesund    weh tun

**5 What is wrong with the person?  What have they injured?  Write the correct German word.**

**a** "Ich kann nicht schreiben."      **e** "Ich war zu lange in der Sonne."

**b** "Ich kann nicht sprechen."       **f** "Ich habe zu viel gegessen."

**c** "Ich kann nicht gehen."          **g** "Die Musik in der Disko war zu laut."

**d** "Ich kann nicht hören."

**6 Find another way of saying these phrases.**

**a** Ich habe einen Schnupfen.      **d** Ich habe sehr hohe Temperatur.

**b** Was ist geschehen?             **e** Ich fühle mich krank.

**c** Achtung!

**7 Sometimes German words are the same as the English word. There are four in this unit.  What are they?**

**8 Sometimes the German and English words are very similar.  Can you find eight from this unit?**

| der Baum | tree | die Garderobe | cloakroom* |
|---|---|---|---|
| der Bungalow | bungalow | die Geschirrspülmaschine | dishwasher |
| der CD-Spieler | CD player | | |
| der Computer | computer | die Haustür | front door |
| der Dachboden | attic* | die Hintertür | back door |
| der Fernseher | TV set | die Kerze | candle* |
| der Flur | hall | die Küche | kitchen |
| der Fön | hair dryer* | die Lampe | lamp |
| der Garten | garden | die Mauer | (outside) wall* |
| der Grasschneider | lawnmower* | die Mikrowelle | microwave |
| der Herd | cooker | die Pflanze | plant |
| der Keller | cellar | die Spülmaschine | dishwasher |
| der Kleiderschrank | wardrobe | die Stereoanlage | stereo unit |
| der Kühlschrank | fridge | die Tiefkühltruhe | deep freeze* |
| der Nachttisch | bedside table | die Toilette | toilet |
| der Rasen | lawn* | die Treppe | stairs |
| der Rasenmäher | lawnmower* | die Tür | door |
| der Schrank | cupboard | die Wand | wall |
| der Sessel | armchair | die Waschmaschine | washing machine |
| der Spiegel | mirror | | |
| der Staubsauger | vacuum cleaner | die Wohnung | flat |
| der Stuhl | chair | die Zentralheizung | central heating |
| der Teppich | carpet | | |
| der Tisch | table | das Bad | bath |
| der Vorhang | curtain | das Badezimmer | bathroom |
| der Wecker | alarm clock | das Bett | bed |
| der Wohnblock | block of flats | das Bild | picture |
| | | das Bügeleisen | iron* |
| die Blume | flower | das Dach | roof* |
| die Decke | ceiling* | das Doppelhaus | semi-detached house |
| die Garage | garage | | |

das Einfamilienhaus detached house
das Esszimmer dining room
das Fenster window
das Gas gas
das Gras grass
das Gebäude building
das Haus house
das Licht light
das Poster poster
das Radio radio
das Reihenhaus terraced house
das Schlafzimmer bedroom
das Sofa sofa, settee
das Telefon telephone
das Videogerät video machine*
das Wohnzimmer living room
das Zimmer room

die Möbel furniture

gießen to pour, to water

draußen outside
drinnen inside
oben upstairs
unten downstairs

**1** Put these things in the room they normally go in.

die Spülmaschine    das Bett    das Bad    der Kühlschrank    der Tisch
die Waschmaschine    der Fernseher    das Auto    der Herd    der Sessel
das Sofa    der Kleiderschrank

**a**  das Badezimmer        _____

**b**  das Esszimmer         _____

**c**  die Küche             _____  _____  _____  _____

**d**  die Garage            _____

**e**  das Schlafzimmer      _____  _____

**f**  das Wohnzimmer        _____  _____  _____

**2** Write down the names of these objects.  Include the gender!

**3** Write down the names of these houses.

**4** Write down words with these endings, giving the number of words asked for:

a Drei mit ......haus

b Vier mit ......zimmer

c Zwei mit ......maschine

d Zwei mit ......schrank

**5** Add another part to these words to make a new word. Then give the meaning of both words.

a die Kleider

b die Maschine

c das Haus

d das Zimmer

e das Dach

**6** Here are some word definitions. What are the words?

a Er steht auf dem Tisch neben dem Bett.

b Ich sehe mich darin.

c Hier gehe ich von unten nach oben.

d Hier ‚wohnt' das Auto.

e Man findet sie im Garten.

f Das Zimmer unter dem Haus.

g Tisch, Stuhl, Sessel, Sofa, usw.

h Er hängt vor dem Fenster.

**7** Where do you find these things in the house? Write down O for 'oben', U for 'unten', B for 'beide' and D for 'draußen'.

a das Badezimmer

b der Keller

c die Pflanze

d der Dachboden

e die Küche

f der Baum

g die Decke

h der Wecker

i der Teppich

**8** Put these words in the order in which you would find them in the house, starting from the top of the house.

| | | |
|---|---|---|
| die Treppe | das Dach | das Schlafzimmer |
| der Flur | der Keller | der Dachboden |

| der Haushalt | household |
| --- | --- |

| die CD | CD |
| --- | --- |
| die Gartenarbeit | gardening |
| die Hausarbeit | housework |
| die Kassette | cassette |
| die Mahlzeit | mealtime |
| die Mittagszeit | midday, lunchtime |
| die Musik | music |

| das Abendessen | evening meal |
| --- | --- |
| das Frühstück | breakfast |
| das Mittagessen | lunch |
| das Radio | radio |

| abräumen | to clear (table) |
| --- | --- |
| abspülen | to wash up |
| abtrocknen | to dry up |
| abwaschen | to wash up |
| anmachen | to turn on (light) |
| aufräumen | to tidy up |
| aufstehen | to get up |
| aufwachen | to wake up |
| ausmachen | to turn off (light) |
| bügeln | to iron |
| decken | to set (the table) |
| duschen | to shower |
| einkaufen | to shop |
| essen | to eat |

| fernsehen | to watch TV |
| --- | --- |
| frühstücken | to have breakfast |
| hören | to hear |
| (sich) kämmen | to comb one's hair* |
| klingeln | to ring (alarm, doorbell) |
| klopfen | to knock* |
| kochen | to cook |
| lesen | to read |
| mähen | to mow* |
| plaudern | to chat |
| putzen | to clean |
| (sich die Zähne) putzen | to clean one's teeth |
| (sich) rasieren | to have a shave* |
| schlafen | to sleep |
| Staub saugen | to vacuum |
| teilen | to share |
| trinken | to drink |
| üben | to practise |
| verlassen | to leave |
| vorbereiten | to prepare |
| waschen | to wash |
| (sich) waschen | to have a wash |
| wecken | to wake someone up |

| eigen | own |
| --- | --- |
| zu Hause | at home |

**1** What are these people doing?  Write down the verbs.

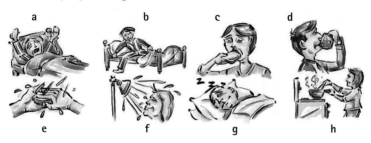

**2** Put these sentences into the correct order.

a  Ich dusche.

b  Ich verlasse das Haus.

c  Ich esse das Mittagessen.

d  Ich wache auf.

e  Der Wecker klingelt.

f  Ich koche das Abendessen.

g  Ich frühstücke.

h  Ich stehe auf.

**3** Where does this happen?  Complete the table.

| a Im Badezimmer | b Im Schlafzimmer | c In der Küche |
|---|---|---|
| | | |
| | | |
| | | |
| | | |

Ich wache auf.    Ich trinke.    Ich dusche.    Ich schlafe.
Ich koche.    Der Wecker klingelt.    Ich esse.    Ich wasche mich.
Ich stehe auf.    Ich putze mir die Zähne.

**4** When do you do this?  Write V for 'vor dem Essen', N for 'nach dem Essen' and B for 'beim Essen'.

abräumen    kochen    abwaschen    decken    abspülen    essen
plaudern    vorbereiten    abtrocknen

## Special Occasions

| | |
|---|---|
| der Geburtstag | birthday |
| der Karneval | carneval |
| der Namenstag | name day* |

| | |
|---|---|
| die Einladung | invitation |
| die Fastenzeit | Lent |
| die Party | party |

| | |
|---|---|
| das Fest | festival |
| das Geschenk | present |

| | |
|---|---|
| ablehnen | to refuse* |
| annehmen | to accept |
| danken | to thank |
| einladen | to invite |
| feiern | to celebrate |

| | |
|---|---|
| gratulieren | to congratulate |
| schenken | to give a present |

| | |
|---|---|
| alles Gute | all the best |
| dankbar | grateful, thankful* |
| Fasching | pre-Lent carnival |
| Fröhliche Weihnachten! | Happy Christmas! |
| Neujahr | New Year |
| Ostern | Easter |
| Pfingsten | Whit* |
| Prost! | Cheers! |
| Silvester | New Year's Eve |
| Weihnachten | Christmas |
| Zum Wohl! | Good health! |

**1** Write down the words suggested by these pictures.

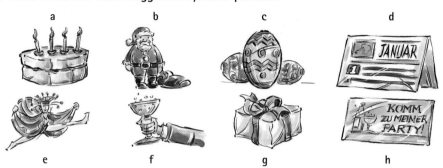

**2** Fill in the gaps in these greetings.

a Alles _____ zum Geburtstag.

b Fröhliche _____!

c Zum _____!

**3** Put these sentences into the correct chronological order.

a Ich habe meinem Freund das Geschenk gegeben.

b Ich bin zur Party gegangen.

c Ich habe die Einladung angenommen.

d Wir haben gut gefeiert.

e Ich habe eine Einladung bekommen.

f Er war sehr dankbar.

g Ich habe ein Geschenk gekauft.

**4** Fill in the missing consonants in these words.

a _ e i _ _ a _ _ _ e _      c _ a _ e _ _ _ a _

b _ _ i _ _ _ _ e _      d _ a _ _ e _ a _

**5** Put these festivals into chronological order, starting on January 1st.

| Weihnachten Fasching Pfingsten Silvester Ostern Neujahr |
| --- |

| | |
|---|---|
| der Sportplatz | sportsground |
| der Tabak | tobacco |
| der Vegetarier | vegetarian |

| | |
|---|---|
| die Gymnastik | gymnastics |
| die Werbung | advertising |

| | |
|---|---|
| das Fett | fat |
| das Fitnesszentrum | fitness centre |
| das Sportzentrum | sports centre |
| das Vitamin | vitamin |

| | |
|---|---|
| abnehmen | to lose weight |
| aufgeben | to give up |
| joggen | to jog |
| rauchen | to smoke |
| (sich) trimmen | to get fit |
| zunehmen | to put on weight |

| | |
|---|---|
| fettig | fatty |
| fit | fit |
| unfit | unfit |
| ungesund | unhealthy |

**1 Are these people fit or unfit?  Write F for fit, U for unfit.**

a  Ich esse viel Gemüse.

b  Ich rauche eine Packung Zigaretten jeden Tag.

c  Ich gehe oft zum Fitnesszentrum.

d  Ich jogge zwanzig Minuten jeden Tag.

e  Ich esse kein fettiges Fleisch.

f  Ich habe das Rauchen aufgegeben.

g  Ich bleibe oft zu Hause und sehe viel fern.

h  Ich habe in der letzten Zeit sehr viel zugenommen.

**2 Solve the anagrams.**

a  cish mitnrme                    e  Wunbreg

b  hebmanne                        f  greetraVi

c  sendgunu                        g  laptoptrzS

**3 Fill in the gaps in these sentences.**

a  Ich rauche nicht.  _____ ist ungesund.

b  Ich esse kein Fleisch.  Ich bin _____.

c  Ich gehe oft zum _____.  Fußball, Laufen, Tennis: ich mache alles.

d  Ich muss _____ _____.  Ich bin so unfit.

e  Ich gehe dreimal in der Woche zum _____: Ich mache viel Gymnastik.

f  Ich esse viel Obst und Gemüse: Da sind viele _____ drin.

g  Fettiges Fleisch: Das ist so _____.

h  Ich habe früher viel Fußball gespielt.  Aber letztes Jahr habe ich es

_____.

| der Apfel | apple | die Banane | banana |
| der Apfelsaft | apple juice | die Birne | pear |
| der Blumenkohl | cauliflower | die Bockwurst | boiled sausage |
| der Essig | vinegar | die Bratwurst | grilled sausage |
| der Fisch | fish | die Butter | butter |
| der Fruchtsaft | fruit juice | die Chips | crisps |
| der Hamburger | hamburger | die Cola | cola |
| der Joghurt | yoghurt | die Currywurst | curried sausage |
| der Kaffee | coffee | die Erdbeere | strawberry |
| der Kakao | cocoa | die Erbse | pea |
| der Käse | cheese | die Himbeere | raspberry |
| der Kaugummi | chewing gum | die Kartoffel | potato |
| der Keks | biscuit | die Karotte | carrot |
| der Kohl | cabbage | die Kirsche | cherry |
| der Kuchen | cake | die Limonade | lemonade |
| der Orangensaft | orange juice | die Margarine | margarine |
| der Pfeffer | pepper | die Marmelade | jam |
| der Pfirsich | peach | die Milch | milk |
| der Reis | rice | die Nahrung | food |
| der Saft | juice | die Orange | orange |
| der Salat | salad | die Pflaume | plum |
| der Schinken | ham | die Pizza | pizza |
| der Senf | mustard | die Pommes | chips |
| der Sprudel | mineral water | die Pommes frites | chips |
| der Tee | tea | die Praline | chocolate (in box) |
| der Toast | toast | | |
| der Wein | wine | die Sahne | cream |
| der Zucker | sugar | die Scheibe | slice |
| | | die Schokolade | chocolate |
| die Apfelsine | orange | die Spaghetti | spaghetti |
| die Aprikose | apricot | die Suppe | soup |
| | | die Süßigkeit | sweet |

| | | | |
|---|---|---|---|
| die Tomate | tomato | das Hähnchen | chicken |
| die Torte | tart, cake | das Kalbfleisch | veal |
| die Vanille | vanilla | das Mineralwasser | mineral water |
| die Weintraube | grape | das Obst | fruit |
| die Wurst | sausage | das Omelette | omelette |
| die Zitrone | lemon | das Rezept | recipe |
| die Zwiebel | onion | das Rindfleisch | beef |
| | | das Salz | salt |
| das Beefsteak | steak | das Schweinefleisch | pork |
| das Bier | beer | das Spiegelei | fried egg |
| das Brot | bread | das Steak | steak |
| das Brötchen | bread roll | das Wasser | water |
| das Butterbrot | sandwich | | |
| das Ei | egg | | |
| das Eis | ice cream | essen | to eat |
| das Fleisch | meat | mischen | to mix |
| das Gemüse | vegetable | schneiden | to cut |
| das Getränk | drink | trinken | to drink |

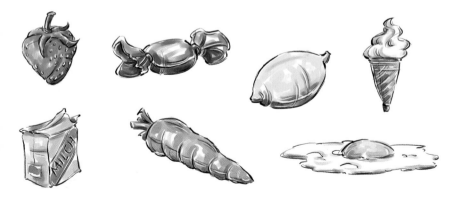

**1** Put the words into the correct column.

| Gemüse | Getränke | Obst |
|--------|----------|------|
|        |          |      |
|        |          |      |
|        |          |      |
|        |          |      |
|        |          |      |

| die Erbse | die Himbeere | der Kaffee | der Kakao | die Karotte |
|---|---|---|---|---|
| die Kartoffel | die Kirsche | der Kohl | der Orangensaft | die Pflaume |
| das Wasser | der Wein | die Weintraube | die Zitrone | die Zwiebel |

**2** Complete the star puzzles.

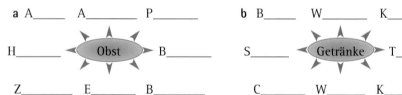

a A_____   A_____   P_____

H_____ ◂ Obst ▸ B_____

Z_____   E_____   B_____

b B_____   W_____   K_____

S_____ ◂ Getränke ▸ T_____

C_____   W_____   K_____

**3** Complete the words by adding to the letters given. Give three words each time.

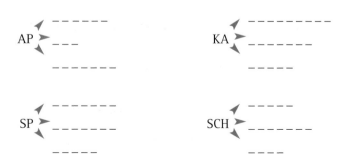

AP ▸ _ _ _ _ _ _
     _ _ _
     _ _ _ _ _ _

KA ▸ _ _ _ _ _ _ _ _
     _ _ _ _ _ _ _
     _ _ _ _

SP ▸ _ _ _ _ _ _
     _ _ _ _ _ _
     _ _ _ _

SCH ▸ _ _ _ _
      _ _ _ _ _ _
      _ _ _ _

**4** Give the genders of these words:

> Kartoffel   Schinken   Birne   Reis   Kohl
> Pfeffer   Salz   Obst   Käse   Wurst

**5** Give German words for the following:

a  two yellow fruits

b  three types of sausage

c  four flavours of ice cream

d  five types of meat

e  six milk products

**6** Complete these pairs.

a  Brot mit _____

b  Fisch mit _____

c  Salz und _____

d  Erdbeeren mit _____

e  Milch und _____

**7** Which food items are being described?

a  Eine Obstsorte: rund, grün oder rot, gut für die Zähne.

b  Eine Gemüsesorte: rund, klein und grün.

c  Eine Obstsorte: gelb, schmeckt sauer.

d  Eine Gemüsesorte: rund; außen braun, innen weiß; man weint, wenn man sie schneidet.

e  Fleisch vom Schwein: rot, oft in Scheiben mit Eiern.

f  Ein Getränk: heiß, mit Milch, Zucker oder Zitrone, Engländer trinken viel davon.

g  Kartoffeln in dünnen Scheiben, in einer Packung.

**8** What are these well known foods? Give the German word and its gender.

a  Golden Delicious   b  Nescafé   c  Cheddar   d  Penguin

e  Basmati   f  Colman's   g  Earl Grey   h  King Edward

| | | | |
|---|---|---|---|
| der Auflauf | soufflé | die Speisekarte | menu |
| der Becher | mug | die Spezialität | speciality |
| der Braten | roast | die Suppe | soup |
| der Champignon | mushroom | die Tasse | cup |
| der Durst | thirst | die Traube | grape |
| der Geruch | smell | die Vorspeise | starter |
| der Geschmack | taste | | |
| der Hunger | hunger | das Besteck | cutlery* |
| der Imbiss | snack | das Bier | beer |
| der Kaffee | coffee | das Eis | ice-cream |
| der Kellner | waiter | das Café | café |
| der Löffel | spoon | das Gasthaus | pub, restaurant |
| der Nachtisch | sweet, dessert | das Geschirr | crockery* |
| der Teller | plate | das Getränk | drink |
| der Tisch | table | das Glas | glass |
| der Topf | pan, dish | das Hauptgericht | main course |
| | | das Kännchen | pot |
| die Bar | bar | das Menü | set menu |
| die Bedienung | service | das Messer | knife |
| die Bohne | bean | das Restaurant | restaurant |
| die Forelle | trout | das Stück | piece |
| die Gabel | fork | das Tagesmenü | menu of the day |
| die Gaststätte | pub, restaurant | das Trinkgeld | tip |
| die Getränkekarte | wine list | das Wiener Schnitzel | veal cutlet, cooked in bread crumbs |
| die Hauptspeise | main course | | |
| die Imbissstube | snack bar | | |
| die Kanne | pot | die Meeresfrüchte | sea food |
| die Kneipe | pub* | | |
| die Portion | portion | bestellen | to order |
| die Schale | bowl | bezahlen | to pay |
| die Selbstbedienung | self service | | |
| die Serviette | serviette | | |

| | |
|---|---|
| probieren | to try |
| reichen | to pass |
| reservieren | to reserve |
| riechen | to smell |
| schmecken | to taste |
| servieren | to serve |
| zahlen | to pay |

| | |
|---|---|
| Das stimmt so | That's okay, keep the change |
| durstig | thirsty |
| Fräulein! | Waitress! |
| Guten Appetit! | Enjoy your meal! |
| Hat's geschmeckt? | Did you enjoy your meal? |
| Herr Ober! | Waiter! |
| hungrig | hungry |
| ich hätte gern ... | I would like ... |
| lecker | tasty |
| Mehrwertsteuer | value added tax (VAT) |
| satt | full, satisfied |
| sauer | sour |
| süß | sweet |
| Zahlen, bitte. | The bill, please. |

## 1 Write down the words for these items.

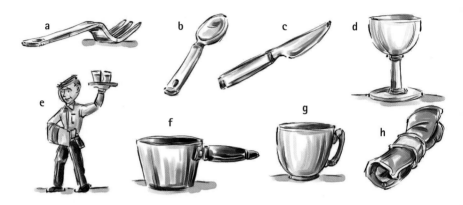

## 2 Match up the words in these two groups and give the meaning of each word.

| Braten | Getränk | Kännchen | Kellner | Nachtisch | schmecken | Vorspeise |
| --- | --- | --- | --- | --- | --- | --- |

| Bier | Eis | Fleisch | Kaffee | lecker | Suppe | Trinkgeld |
| --- | --- | --- | --- | --- | --- | --- |

## 3 Put these phrases into chronological order as you would use them in a restaurant.

**a** Herr Ober, zahlen bitte.

**b** Ja, ich bin satt.

**c** Ich nehme das Menü, bitte.

**d** Das stimmt so.

**e** Auf Wiedersehen.

**f** Guten Tag. Ein Tisch für zwei Personen, bitte.

**g** Darf ich die Speisekarte sehen?

**h** Hat's geschmeckt?

**i** Guten Appetit!

**4 Complete the words by adding to the letters given. Give three words every time.**

**5 Put these words into the order in which they would occur in a restaurant.**

a bestellen    b bezahlen    c Hauptgericht    d Nachtisch

e Speisekarte    f Trinkgeld    g Vorspeise

**6 Write down the German for:**

a three places to eat

b three containers for drinks

c three courses in a meal

**7 Solve these anagrams.**

a stepSreakie

b rerobenip

c Gräntek

d eisVespor

e meGschack

|  |  |
|--------|---------|
| der Basketball | basketball |
| der Besuch | visit |
| der Comic | comic |
| der Dokumentarfilm | documentary film |
| der Eintritt | entrance fee |
| der Fan | fan |
| der Film | film |
| der Fotoapparat | camera |
| der Freizeitpark | theme park |
| der Fußball | football |
| der Horrorfilm | horror film |
| der Krimi | crime film/book |
| der Liebesfilm | love film |
| der Rollschuh | roller skate |
| der Roman | novel |
| der Sänger | singer |
| der Schauspieler | actor |
| der Sitz | seat |
| der Spaß | fun |
| der Sport | sport |
| der Tanz | dance |
| der Titel | title |
| der Untertitel | subtitle |
| der Verein | club, team |
| der Volleyball | volleyball |
| der Walkman | walkman |
| der Wettbewerb | competition |
| der Wintersport | winter sport |
| der Zettel | piece of paper, note |

|  |  |
|--------|---------|
| die Disko | disco |
| die Freizeit | free time |
| die Gruppe | group |
| die Kamera | camera |
| die Mannschaft | team |
| die Musik | music |
| die Popmusik | pop music |
| die Sendung | broadcast |
| die Serie | series |
| die Tagesschau | TV news |
| die Vorstellung | performance |
| die Zeitschrift | magazine |
| die Zeitung | newspaper |

|  |  |
|--------|---------|
| das Endspiel | final |
| das Foto | photo |
| das Freibad | open-air swimming pool |
| das Hallenbad | indoor swimming pool |
| das Hobby | hobby |
| das Instrument | instrument |
| das Interesse | interest |
| das Klavier | piano |
| das Konzert | concert |
| das Lied | song |
| das Mitglied | member |
| das Picknick | picnic |
| das Programm | programme |
| das Schwimmbad | swimming pool |
| das Spiel | game |

| | | | | |
|---|---|---|---|---|
| das Theaterstück | play | Rollschuh laufen | to rollerskate |
| das Videospiel | video game | sammeln | to collect |
| | | Schlittschuh laufen | to skate |
| die Nachrichten | news | schwimmen | to swim |
| | | segeln | to sail |
| ausverkauft | sold out | Ski fahren | to ski |
| im Freien | in the open air | spazieren gehen | to go for a walk |
| | | spielen | to play |
| Badminton | badminton | tanzen | to dance |
| Basketball | basketball | tauchen | to dive* |
| Fußball | football | trainieren | to train |
| Pop | pop | treffen | to meet |
| Schach | chess | üben | practise |
| Tennis | tennis | wandern | to walk, hike |
| Tischtennis | tabletennis | | |
| Volleyball | volleyball | klassisch | classical |
| | | langweilig | boring |
| angeln | to fish | spannend | exciting |
| ausgehen | to go out | | |
| besuchen | to visit | | |
| faulenzen | to laze about | | |
| fernsehen | to watch TV | | |
| fotografieren | to photograph | | |
| gewinnen | to win | | |
| grillen | to barbecue* | | |
| (sich) interessieren für | to be interested in* | | |
| kegeln | to bowl | | |
| lesen | to read | | |
| programmieren | to programme | | |
| Rad fahren | to cycle | | |
| reiten | to ride (horse) | | |

**1** What are these people doing?  Write down the verbs.

**2** Match up five pairs of words which go together from this list.

> das Schwimmbad    das Hobby    üben    treffen    das Hallenbad
> trainieren    die Gruppe    ausgehen    die Freizeit    die Mannschaft

**3** Write down:

a three things to read

b four indoor sports or games

c five words to do with music

d six words to do with the cinema

**4** When you do these sports, how do you play?  Write M for 'in einer Mannschaft', write P for 'mit einem Partner' and write A for 'allein'.

> Angeln    Badminton    Basketball    Fußball    Rad fahren    Reiten
> Schach    Ski fahren    Schwimmen    Tanzen    Tennis
> Tischtennis    Volleyball

**5** Add extra parts to make longer words. (The number tells you how many longer words to write.)  Write down the meaning of all the words.

a Theater (1)

b Tennis (1)

c Ball (3)

d Schuh (1)

e Titel (1)

f Spieler (1)

g Bad (3)

h Spiel (2)

**Complete the answers by writing down the correct verb.**

| programmieren | sammeln | sehen | schwimmen | fotografieren |

> Remember the ending for 'ich': ........e.

**a** Hast du einen Computer? Ja, ich _____ jeden Abend.

**b** Gehst du oft ins Kino?  Ja, ich _____ gern Filme.

**c** Gehst du ins Hallenbad? Ja,  ich _____ sehr gern.

**d** Hast du einen Fotoapparat? Ja, ich _____meine Familie.

**e** Hast du ein Hobby? Ja, ich _____ Briefmarken.

**Give the past participles for:**

**a** schwimmen      **c** gewinnen      **e** lesen

**b** besuchen      **d** treffen

**Now write the correct words in these sentences:**

**a** Ich habe meine Oma _____

**b** Ich habe im Schwimmbad _____

**c** Ich habe die Zeitschrift _____

**d** Ich habe meine Freunde _____

**e** Die Mannschaft hat im Endspiel _____

**Where do these words belong? Write L for 'lesen', M for 'Musik' and K for 'Kino'.**

| der Comic    der Eintritt    der Horrorfilm    das Klavier    die Zeitung
das Konzert    der Krimi    der Untertitel    das Lied
der Roman    der Sänger    der Schauspieler    die Vorstellung
der Walkman    die Zeitschrift |

| | | | | |
|---|---|---|---|---|
| der Charakter | character | | brav | well-behaved* |
| der Mensch | person, human being | | doof | stupid |
| | | | dumm | stupid |
| der Streit | argument, quarrel | | ehrlich | honest |
| | | | erfolgreich | successful |
| | | | ernst | serious* |
| die Angst | fear | | faul | lazy |
| die Freude | joy | | fleißig | hard-working |
| die Liebe | love | | frech | cheeky* |
| die Nerven | nerves | | freundlich | friendly |
| die Persönlichkeit | personality | | geduldig | patient |
| | | | geschwätzig | talkative |
| das Verhältnis | relationship | | glücklich | happy |
| das Vertrauen | trust* | | gut gelaunt | good-humoured |
| | | | hilfsbereit | ready to help |
| lachen | to laugh | | höflich | polite |
| lächeln | to smile* | | humorlos | humourless |
| lügen | to lie | | intelligent | intelligent |
| streiten | to argue | | interessant | interesting |
| (sich) verstehen | to get on with someone | | komisch | funny |
| weinen | to cry | | klug | clever |
| | | | launisch | moody |
| ähnlich | similar* | | laut | loud |
| aktiv | active | | lebendig | lively |
| allein | alone | | lebhaft | lively |
| altmodisch | old-fashioned | | leise | quiet |
| amüsant | amusing | | lieb | nice, kind |
| arm | poor | | lustig | funny |
| berühmt | famous | | nett | nice |
| blöd | silly, stupid | | optimistisch | optimistic |
| böse | angry | | pessimistisch | pessimistic |

| | | | |
|---|---|---|---|
| praktisch | practical | ungeduldig | impatient |
| pünktlich | prompt | unglücklich | unhappy |
| ruhig | quiet | unhöflich | impolite |
| schüchtern | shy | unzufrieden | discontented |
| streng | strict | verantwortlich | responsible* |
| sympathisch | sympathetic | vorsichtig | careful |
| traurig | sad | witzig | funny |
| treu | loyal* | zufrieden | content |
| typisch | typical | zuverlässig | reliable* |
| unfreundlich | unfriendly | | |

## 1 What adjectives describe these people?

## 2 Are these adjectives positive (+) or negative ( - )?

a  doof

b  launisch

c  nett

d  unhöflich

e  faul

f  ungeduldig

g  freundlich

h  brav

**3 Write down:**

**a** two words ending in 'ant'

**b** four words ending in 'lich'

**c** six words ending in 'ig'

**4 Write the opposites of these words.**

**a** dumm

**b** laut

**c** glücklich

**d** faul

**e** ernst

**f** optimistisch

**g** geduldig

**h** geschwätzig

**5 Write an adjective describing someone's personality for each letter of the alphabet.**

(There are no words for the letters C, J, M, Q, X, Y.)

**6 Use an adjective to fill the gaps in these sentences.**

**a** Er war sehr _____. Sein Gesicht war rot.

**b** Er bleibt bis elf Uhr im Bett. Er ist sehr _____.

**c** Er spricht nicht viel. Er ist sehr _____.

**d** Die Familie ist _____: Sie hat nicht viel Geld.

**e** Sylvester Stallone ist ein _____ Schauspieler.

**f** Er lacht nicht viel. Er ist sehr _____.

**g** Sie trägt nie moderne Kleider. Sie ist sehr _____.

**h** Er lügt nie. Er ist sehr _____.

| | |
|---|---|
| der Abend | evening |
| der Augenblick | moment |
| der Moment | moment |
| der Monat | month |
| der Morgen | morning |
| der Nachmittag | afternoon |
| der Punkt | point, dot |
| der Tag | day |
| der Treffpunkt | meeting place* |
| der Vormittag | morning |

| | |
|---|---|
| die Minute | minute |
| die Sekunde | second |
| die Uhr | hour |
| die Woche | week |
| die Zeit | time |

| | |
|---|---|
| das Handy | mobile phone |
| das Datum | date |
| das Jahr | year |
| das Mal | time, occasion |
| das Wochenende | weekend |

| | |
|---|---|
| ausmachen | to arrange |
| duzen | to call someone 'du' |
| (sich) freuen | to be pleased |
| (sich) freuen auf | to look forward to |
| hereinkommen | to come in |
| hoffen | to hope |
| kennen | to know |

| | |
|---|---|
| mitkommen | to come, go with someone |
| (sich) setzen | to sit down |
| siezen | to call someone 'Sie' |
| treffen | to meet |
| (sich) verabschieden | to take one's leave |
| vorstellen | to introduce |
| (sich) vorstellen | to introduce oneself |
| stattfinden | to take place |
| vorhaben (etwas) | to have (something) 'on'* |

| | |
|---|---|
| abgemacht | agreed |
| auf Wiederhören | goodbye (on phone) |
| auf Wiedersehen | goodbye |
| danke | thank you |
| Grüß Gott | hello (Bavarian) |
| Hallo | hello |
| herzlich willkommen | welcome |
| hoffentlich | I hope that |
| Lust haben | to want |
| Servus | hello, goodbye (S. Germany) |
| um halb sieben | at half past six |
| um sechs Uhr | at six o'clock |
| um Viertel nach sechs | at a quarter past six |
| Wie geht's? | How are you? |

| | | | |
|---|---|---|---|
| Montag | Monday | Januar | January |
| Dienstag | Tuesday | Februar | February |
| Mittwoch | Wednesday | März | March |
| Donnerstag | Thursday | April | April |
| Freitag | Friday | Mai | May |
| Samstag | Saturday | Juni | June |
| Sonnabend | Saturday (N. Germany) | Juli | July |
| | | August | August |
| Sonntag | Sunday | September | September |
| | | Oktober | October |
| montags, usw. | on Mondays, etc. | November | November |
| | | Dezember | December |

| | |
|---|---|
| bis | until |
| gestern | yesterday |
| heute | today |
| jede(n) | every |
| jetzt | now |
| letzt | last |
| manchmal | sometimes |
| Mittag | midday |
| Mitternacht | midnight |
| morgen | tomorrow |
| nachher | afterwards |
| nächst | next |
| nun | now |
| sofort | immediately |
| täglich | daily |
| übermorgen | day after tomorrow |
| vorgestern | day before yesterday |

| | |
|---|---|
| Der wievielte ist heute? | What's the date today? |
| Treffen wir uns um... | Let's meet at |
| Wie spät ist es? | What time is it? |
| Wie viel Uhr ist es? | What time is it? |

**1** Put these phrases into chronological order. Start with the one furthest in the past.

> übermorgen   gestern   nächste Woche   letzte Woche
> nächstes Jahr   morgen   vorgestern   heute

**2** Write down the day and date in words:

a  Sa.  11.1

b  Mi.  22.3

c  Do.  19.5

d  So.  8.12

e  Fr.  30.11

f  Di.  15.10

g  Mo.  14.7

h  Do.  12.8

**3** Answer these vocabulary sums.

a   eine Sekunde x 60 =

b   ein Monat x 12 =

c   ein Tag x 7 =

d   eine Stunde x 24 =

e   Samstag + Sonntag =

f   eine Woche x 4 =

**4** Coming or going?  When would you say these phrases?  Write A for when you arrive and L for when you leave.

a  Guten Morgen.

b  Bis morgen, also.

c  Herzlich willkommen.

d  Auf Wiedersehen.

e  Es freut mich, Sie kennenzulernen.

f  Schönes Wochenende.

g  Wie geht's?

h  Grüß Gott.

**5** Write two German words for:

a  Saturday

b  morning

c  moment

d  now

e  every day

**6 Solve these word puzzles.**

 **a** ein Tag mit ‚schlechtem Wetter‘

 **b** ein Tag ohne ‚Tag‘

 **c** ein Tag, wo man immer ‚Sonne‘ hat

 **d** Ist alles ‚kostenlos‘ an diesem Tag?

**7 Solve these anagrams. Each word starts with the letter in the middle.**

**a**
| a | c | h |
|---|---|---|
| a | **m** | n |
| m | l |   |

**b**
| n | t | h | f |
|---|---|---|---|
|   | f | **h** | c |
| l | o | i | e |

**c**
| o | h | e |
|---|---|---|
| a | **v** | r |
| b | n |   |

**d**
| h | i | g | m |
|---|---|---|---|
| t | **N** | a |   |
| a | t | c |   |

**e**
| a | e | o |
|---|---|---|
| d | **S** | n |
| n | b | n |

**8 Add another part to make a longer word. Give the meaning of both words.**

 **a** Abend

 **b** kommen

 **c** Mittag

 **d** morgen

 **e** gestern

 **f** Woche

 **g** finden

 **h** Punkt

**9 Solve these dingbats.**

 **a** gen
   mor

 **b** mittag der

 **c** w o c h e n e n d e

|  |  |  |  |
|---|---|---|---|
| der Ausverkauf | sale* | die Dose | tin |
| der Cent | cent | die Drogerie | chemist |
| der Einkaufswagen | shopping trolley | die Etage | floor |
| der Euro | euro (money) | die Flasche | bottle |
| der Franken | franc (Switzerland) | die Fleischerei | butchers |
|  |  | die Geschäftszeit | opening hours |
| der Geldbeutel | purse | die Kasse | cash desk |
| der Karton | carton | die Konditorei | cake shop |
| der Korb | basket | die Kreditkarte | credit card |
| der Kunde | customer | die Liste | list |
| der Laden | shop | die Metzgerei | butchers |
| der Liter | liter | die Öffnungszeit | opening time |
| der Markt | market | die Packung | packet |
| der Marktplatz | market place | die Quittung | receipt* |
| der Preis | price | die Schachtel | box |
| der Rappen | rappen (Switzerland) | die Scheibe | slice |
| der Scheck | cheque | die Schreibwarenhandlung | stationers |
| der Schein | bank note | die Tasche | shopping bag |
| der Stock | floor | die Tube | tube |
| der Supermarkt | supermarket | die Tüte | bag |
| der Tabakladen | tobacconists | die Verkäuferin | salesperson |
| der Verkäufer | salesperson |  |  |
| der Umschlag | envelope |  |  |
| der Zentimeter | centimetre | das Angebot | offer |
|  |  | das Bargeld | cash |
| die Abteilung | department | das Bonbon | sweet |
| die Apotheke | chemist | das Dutzend | dozen |
| die Auswahl | choice* | das Erdgeschoss | ground floor |
| die Bäckerei | bakery | das Fenster | window |
| die Brieftasche | wallet | das Geschäft | shop |
| die Buchhandlung | bookshop | das Gramm | gram |

| | | | | |
|---|---|---|---|---|
| das Kaufhaus | department store | | ausverkauft | sold out |
| das Kilo | kilo | | billig | cheap |
| das Lebensmittelgeschäft | grocers | | ein bisschen | a bit |
| das Päckchen | packet | | ein paar | a few |
| das Paket | packet | | ein wenig | a little |
| das Portemonnaie | purse | | einige | some |
| das Pfund | pound (weight, English money) | | genug | enough |
| das Regal | shelf* | | geöffnet | open |
| das Schaufenster | display window | | geschlossen | closed |
| das Stück | piece | | gratis | free |
| das Süßwarengeschäft | sweet shop | | kostenlos | free |
| das Untergeschoss | basement | | offen | open |
| | | | preiswert | value for money |
| die Lebensmittel | groceries | | pro | each |
| die Schreibwaren | stationery | | teuer | dear |
| die Tabakwaren | tobacco goods | | wie viel | how much |
| | | | wie viele | how many |

| | |
|---|---|
| ausgeben | to spend |
| bezahlen | to pay (for) |
| geben | to give |
| kaufen | to buy |
| kosten | to cost |
| öffnen | to open |
| schließen | to close |
| verkaufen | to sell |

**1** Write down the names of these items.

**2** What are these items? Write C for currency, W for weight or M for a measure. Watch out! One of the words has two answers!

a Gramm    b Liter    c Franken    d Euro    e Zentimeter    f Pfund
g Cent    h Rappen    i Kilo

**3** In which shop would you buy these items?

a das Brot    b der Umschlag    c das Buch    d der Kuchen
e das Fleisch    f die Butter    g das Bonbon    h die Zigarette
i die Tabletten

**4** Fill in the gaps in this text.

Ich bin in den Supermarkt gegangen. Das Geschäft ist von 9 Uhr bis 7 Uhr
**a** _____. Am Eingang habe ich einen **b** _____ genommen. Ich
gehe gern in dieses Geschäft: Die **c** _____ ist immer groß. Ich habe eine
**d** _____ Milch, eine **e** _____ Suppe und ein **f** _____ Eier gekauft.
Ich konnte keine Chips kaufen: Das **g** _____ war leer. In der
Gemüse **h**_____ habe ich ein **i** _____ Kartoffeln gekauft. Ich
habe an der **j** _____ bezahlt. Die Kassiererin hat mir die
**k** _____ gegeben. Alles hat nur €3 gekostet. Ich finde, das ist sehr
**l** _____. Ich habe alles in meine **m** _____ getan und dann bin
ich nach Hause gegangen.

**5** Add to these words to form a longer word. Write down the meaning of both
words.

**a** Tasche    **b** Markt    **c** Karte    **d** kaufen    **e** Fenster
**f** Zeit    **g** Haus    **h** Geld    **i** geben

**6** Make ten words from these parts of words. Each word has three parts.

| | | | | | | | | | |
|---|---|---|---|---|---|---|---|---|---|
| ab | aus | buch | ein | fen | ge | ger | geschäft | hand | kauf |
| kaufs | kosten | lebens | los | lung | metz | mittel | ei | schau |
| | schoss | ster | teil | ung | unter | ver | wagen | |

**7** Write down:

**a** the currency of Austria (two words)

**b** the currency of Germany  (two words)

**c** the currency of Switzerland (two words)

**d** three ways of making a payment

**e** three containers

**f** three weights

| | | | | |
|---|---|---|---|---|
| der Anzug | suit* | | die Größe | size |
| der Badeanzug | swimming costume | | die Hose | trousers |
| | | | die Jacke | jacket |
| der Gürtel | belt | | die Jeans | jeans |
| der Handschuh | glove | | die Kette | chain, necklace |
| der Hut | hat | | die Kleidung | clothing |
| der Knopf | button | | die Krawatte | tie |
| der Lippenstift | lipstick | | die kurze Hose | shorts |
| der Mantel | coat | | die Mode | fashion |
| der Modezeichner | fashion designer* | | die Mütze | cap* |
| | | | die Sandale | sandal |
| der Ohrring | earring | | die Seide | silk |
| der Pulli | pullover | | die Shorts | shorts |
| der Pullover | pullover | | die Socke | sock |
| der Pyjama | pyjamas | | die Wolle | wool |
| der Regenmantel | raincoat | | | |
| der Regenschirm | umbrella | | das Hemd | shirt |
| der Ring | ring | | das Kleid | dress |
| der Rock | skirt | | das Leder | leather |
| der Schal | scarf | | das Make-up | make-up |
| der Schlafanzug | pyjamas | | das Paar | pair |
| der Schlips | tie | | das Parfum | perfume |
| der Schmuck | jewellery | | das Piercing | piercing |
| der Schuh | shoe | | das Sweatshirt | sweatshirt |
| der Stiefel | boot* | | das Taschentuch | handkerchief |
| | | | das Trikot | football shirt |
| die Armbanduhr | wristwatch* | | das T-Shirt | t-shirt |
| die Baumwolle | cotton | | | |
| die Badehose | swimming trunks | | die Klamotten | clothes (slang)* |
| | | | die Lippen | lips |
| die Bluse | blouse | | | |
| die Farbe | colour | | | |

| | | | |
|---|---|---|---|
| anprobieren | to try on | grau | grey |
| anziehen | to put on | grün | green |
| ausziehen | to take off | hell | light |
| passen | to fit, to suit | lila | lilac |
| stehen | to suit | modern | modern |
| tragen | to wear | modisch | fashionable* |
| umtauschen | to exchange* | orange | orange |
| umziehen | to change | rein | pure* |
| vergleichen | to compare | rosa | pink |
| vorziehen | to prefer | rot | red |
| | | schick | chic, fashionable |
| bequem | comfortable | | |
| blau | blue | schwarz | black |
| braun | brown | wasserdicht | waterproof |
| bunt | bright, colourful | wasserfest | waterproof |
| | | weiß | white |
| dunkel | dark | | |
| echt | genuine* | Welche Größe haben Sie? | What size do you take? |
| gelb | yellow | | |
| gold | gold | | |

**1** Write down the names of these items of clothing.

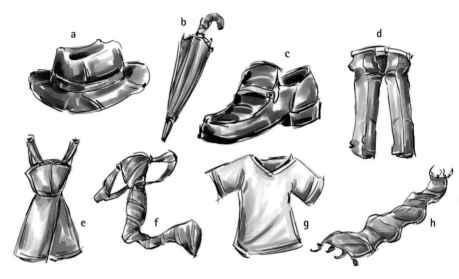

**2** Add another part to each word to make a new word. Write down the meaning of both words.

**a** Anzug    **b** Mantel    **c** Wolle    **d** Lippen    **e** Hose
**f** Schuh    **g** Ring

**3** Write down:

**a** two words for 'tie'

**b** four colours beginning with 'g'

**c** four items of clothes where the English word is the same as the German word

**d** four verbs ending in 'ziehen'

**4** What clothes would you wear on these parts of the body?

**a** die Hand    **b** der Kopf    **c** das Ohr    **d** der Hals
**e** der Fuß    **f** die Beine

**Fill in the missing words in these sentences.**

**a** Kann ich bitte diese Jacke _____?

**b** Welche _____ haben Sie?

**c** Ich möchte schwimmen, aber ich habe meine _____ vergessen.

**d** Es regnet. Nimm deinen _____ und deinen _____ mit.

**e** Welche _____ ziehst du vor? Gelb oder grün?

**f** Die Schuhe sind nicht _____. Sie sind zu klein.

**g** Du wirst nicht nass. Die Jacke ist _____.

**Complete the words by adding to the given letter(s). Give three words every time.**

**Write down the colour(s) of the following:**

**a** das Gras
**b** eine Zitrone
**c** ein Elefant
**d** die Ampel (drei)
**e** der Trikot von Manchester United
**f** ein Ei (zwei)
**g** die britische Flagge (drei)
**h** die deutsche Flagge
**i** die österreichische Flagge
**j** Sahne

| | | | |
|---|---|---|---|
| der Abfall | rubbish, waste | das Problem | problem |
| der Abfalleimer | waste paper basket | das Pfand | deposit (on bottle) |
| der Alkohol | alcohol | das Recycling | re-cycling |
| der Container | bottle bank | | |
| der Dieb | thief | die Abgase | exhaust fumes |
| der Drogensüchtige | drug addict | | |
| der Lärm | noise | | |
| der Müll | rubbish | aufgeben | to give up |
| der Vandalismus | vandalism | ausgeben | to spend |
| | | sparen | to save |
| die Arbeitslosigkeit | unemployment | stehlen | to steal |
| die Droge | drug | trennen | to separate |
| die Energie | energy | wegwerfen | to throw away |
| die Flasche | bottle | | |
| die Gewalt | violence | aktuell | topical |
| die Graffiti | graffiti | betrunken | drunk |
| die Luft | air | obdachlos | homeless |
| die Mehrwegflasche | returnable bottle* | sauber | clean |
| die Mülltonne | dustbin | schmutzig | dirty |
| die Obdachlosigkeit | homelessness | umweltfreundlich | environmentall friendly |
| die Pfandflasche | returnable bottle (with deposit) | | |
| die Politik | politics | | |
| die Süchtigkeit | addiction | | |
| die Umwelt | environment | | |
| die Umweltverschmutzung | environmental pollution | | |
| die Welt | world | | |

**1** **What social issues are being described in these sentences?**

a  Man hat alle Fenster in der Schule kaputtgeschlagen.

b  Man schreibt an Mauern, Briefkästen, usw.

c  Zu viele junge Leute werden betrunken.

d  Papier, leere Flaschen, Dosen, usw. liegen auf der Straße.

e  Wir bringen unsere Flaschen und Dosen immer zum Container.

f  Es gibt zu viele Autos auf unseren Straßen.

g  Viele Leute haben kein Haus: Sie schlafen auf der Straße.

h  Viele junge Leute bekommen heute keine Stelle.

i  Musik, Autos, Flugzeuge, es ist alles so laut.

**2** **Add another part to each word to make a longer word. Write down the meaning of both words.**

a  Abfall    b  Müll    c  Umwelt    d  Flasche    e  werfen    f  geben

**3** **Fill in the missing words in these sentences.**

a  Warum werfen die Leute das Papier nicht in den _____?

b  Die Luft ist heute so _____.

c  Mach das Licht aus! Wir müssen Energie _____.

d  Die Deutschen müssen den Müll _____.

e  Ein _____ hat mein Geld gestohlen.

f  Rauchen ist ungesund. Du solltest es _____.

g  Er schläft auf einer Bank im Park. Er ist _____.

h  Zu viele Leute kaufen Cola in Dosen. Sie sollten _____ kaufen.

**4** **Find eight words in this 'chain'. Write down their meanings.**

idasauberiotndiebohenergieotaweltämlufteraktuellootergewaltumlärm

| | | | |
|---|---|---|---|
| der Bauer | farmer, builder | das Holz | wood |
| der Beginn | beginning | das Plastik | plastic |
| der Besitzer | owner | das Viertel | quarter |
| der Frühling | spring | das Volk | people |
| der Gott | god | | |
| der Grund | reason | abholen | to fetch |
| der Herbst | autumn | ansehen | to look at (closely) |
| der Nachteil | disadvantage | | |
| der Plan | plan | aufmachen | to open |
| der Sommer | summer | aussprechen | to pronounce |
| der Unterschied | difference | bauen | to build |
| der Vorteil | advantage | bedeuten | to mean |
| der Winter | winter | begleiten | to accompany |
| | | bekommen | to get |
| die Art | kind, sort | brauchen | to need |
| die Aussprache | pronunciation | denken (an) | to think (of) |
| die Erlaubnis | permission | drehen | to turn |
| die Idee | idea | dürfen | to be allowed |
| die Meinung | opinion | (sich) entscheiden | to decide |
| die Menge | crowd, a lot | (sich) entschuldigen | to apologise |
| die Pflicht | duty | erzählen | to tell (story) |
| die Runde | round (of competition) | geben | to give |
| | | gehören | to belong |
| die Schwierigkeit | difficulty | (sich) gewöhnen an | to get used to |
| die Sorte | sort, kind | glauben | to believe, thin |
| die Sprache | language | haben | to have |
| die Stille | silence | heben | to lift |
| die Verantwortung | responsibility | können | to be able |
| die Vergangenheit | past | lassen | to leave (behin |
| die Wahl | choice | laufen | to run |
| | | Leid tun (Es tut mir Leid.) | to be sorry (I'm sorry.) |
| das Gegenteil | opposite | | |

| | | | |
|---|---|---|---|
| leihen | to lend | wiederholen | to repeat |
| machen | to make, do | wissen | to know |
| meinen | to think, have an opinion | wollen | to want |
| | | wünschen | to wish |
| messen | to measure | zeigen | to show |
| mitnehmen | to take with one | ziehen | to pull |
| | | zumachen | to close |
| mögen | to like | | |
| müssen | to have to, must | angenehm | pleasant |
| passieren | to happen | ausgezeichnet | excellent |
| sagen | to say | beschäftigt | busy |
| schaden | to harm, damage | besser | better |
| | | breit | broad, wide |
| schieben | to push | einzeln | single |
| schützen | to protect | eng | narrow |
| sehen | to see | erlaubt | allowed |
| sein | to be | fabelhaft | fabulous |
| sitzen | to sit | fantastisch | fantastic |
| sollen | to ought to, should | fest | firm |
| | | falsch | wrong |
| sprechen | to speak | frisch | fresh |
| stehen | to stand | furchtbar | dreadful, terrible |
| steigen | to climb | | |
| sterben | to die | hart | hard |
| stimmen | to be right | herrlich | splendid |
| tun | to do | hervorragend | splendid |
| verbringen | to spend time | hoch | high |
| vergessen | to forget | kaputt | broken |
| verlieren | to lose | kompliziert | complicated |
| verschließen | to lock | langsam | slow |
| versuchen | to try | leer | empty |
| weitermachen | to continue | mies | awful |

| | | | |
|---|---|---|---|
| müde | tired | beide | both |
| neu | new | besonders | especially |
| nötig | necessary | (ein) bisschen | (a) bit |
| nützlich | useful | d.h. (das heißt) | i.e. (that is) |
| nutzlos | useless | da | there, as |
| öffentlich | public | damals | then |
| richtig | right, correct | damit | so that |
| scharf | sharp, hot (taste) | dann | then |
| schlecht | bad | dass | that |
| schlimm | bad | dieser | this |
| schmal | narrow | diesmal | this time |
| schnell | quick, fast | doch | but yes |
| schrecklich | dreadful | dort | there |
| schwierig | difficult | egal | equal |
| sportlich | sporting | endlich | at last |
| still | quiet | es geht | it's OK |
| toll | great | es gibt | there is |
| voll | full | etwa | about |
| wichtig | important | etwas | something |
| wunderbar | wonderful | fast | almost |
| | | genau | exactly |
| | | gerade | just, straight |
| aber | but | gewöhnlich | usually |
| alles | everything | halb | half |
| als | as, when | heutzutage | nowadays |
| also | therefore | hier | here |
| am besten | best | immer | always |
| am liebsten | best | immer noch | still |
| auch | also | in Ordnung | in order |
| außerdem | furthermore, also | im Voraus | in advance |
| bald | soon | jemand | someone |

| | | | |
|---|---|---|---|
| klasse | great | überall | everywhere |
| leider | unfortunately | unbedingt | absolutely |
| Lieblings... | favourite ... | unmöglich | impossible |
| man | one, 'they' | unterwegs | on the way |
| mehr | more | usw. | etc. |
| mehrere | several | Verzeihung! | Sorry! |
| möglich | possible | vielleicht | perhaps |
| natürlich | naturally, of course | völlig | completely |
| | | vorher | previously |
| neulich | recently | wahrscheinlich | probably |
| nicht mehr | no longer | wann | when |
| nichts | nothing | warum | why |
| nie | never | was | what |
| niemand | no-one | was für | what kind of |
| noch einmal | again | weil | because |
| noch nicht | not yet | wenig | few |
| normalerweise | usually | wenn | whenever, if |
| nur | only | wer | who |
| ob | whether | wie | how |
| oder | or | Wie, bitte? | Pardon? |
| plötzlich | suddenly | wieder | again |
| prima | great | wirklich | really |
| schon | already | woher | where from |
| selbst | even, self | wohin | where to |
| selten | rarely | z.B. (zum Beispiel) | e.g. (for example) |
| sicher | safe, sure, certainly | | |
| | | ziemlich | rather |
| so | thus | zu Ende | over |
| so dass | so that | zurück | back |
| sogar | even | zusammen | together |
| sonst | otherwise | | |
| spitze | great | | |

If you can learn these simple rules they will help you form the plurals of most of the German nouns that you will meet in an examination.

## 1 Masculine nouns add Umlaut + 'e'

e.g.　der Fuß　die Füße　　　　der Kopf　die Köpfe

If no Umlaut is possible, just add 'e'

e.g.　der Tisch　die Tische　　　der Brief　die Briefe

**Exceptions**

der Arm　die Arme　　　　der Besuch　die Besuche

der Hund　die Hunde　　　der Monat　die Monate

der Schuh　die Schuhe　　der Tag　die Tage

**and**

der Mann　die Männer　　der Wald　die Wälder

## 2 Feminine nouns add 'n' or 'en'

e.g.　die Frau　die Frauen　　die Tasche　die Taschen

Some feminine nouns add Umlaut + 'e'

e.g.　die Bank　die Bänke　　　die Hand　die Hände

die Kuh　die Kühe　　　　die Maus　die Mäuse

die Nacht　die Nächte　　die Stadt　die Städte

die Wand　die Wände　　die Wurst　die Würste

**Exceptions**

die Mutter　die Mütter　　　　die Tochter　die Töchter

## 3 Neuter nouns add Umlaut + 'er'

e.g.　das Buch　die Bücher　　das Glas　die Gläser

If no Umlaut is possible, just add 'e'

e.g.　das Heft　die Hefte　　　das Pferd　die Pferde

**Exceptions**

| | | | |
|---|---|---|---|
| das Bild | die Bilder | das Ei | die Eier |
| das Jahr | die Jahre | das Kind | die Kinder |

**Masculine and neuter nouns ending in –el, -er, -chen and –lein DON'T CHANGE.**

e.g.   der Füller   die Füller        das Fenster     die Fenster

der Schlüssel   die Schlüssel        das Mädchen     die Mädchen

**Exceptions**

| | | | |
|---|---|---|---|
| der Garten | die Gärten | der Mantel | die Mäntel |
| der Vogel | die Vögel | der Vater | die Väter |
| der Bruder | die Brüder | der Apfel | die Äpfel |
| der Laden | die Läden | | |

**'Weak' masculine nouns add 'n' or 'en'**

e.g.   der Herr   die Herren        der Junge   die Jungen

der Mensch   die Menschen        der Polizist   die Polizisten

der Student   die Studenten

**Foreign neuters add 's'**

e.g.   das Auto   die Autos        das Baby   die Babys

das Kino   die Kinos

**These five neuter nouns add 'n' or 'en'**

| | | | |
|---|---|---|---|
| das Auge | die Augen | das Bett | die Betten |
| das Ende | die Enden | das Hemd | die Hemden |
| das Ohr | die Ohren | | |

## Activities

Write down the plurals of these nouns. Try applying the rules to other words
that you have learned in this book.

| | | |
|---|---|---|
| das Haus | der Sohn | der Mann |
| die Blume | die Zeitung | der Füller |
| der Junge | der Baum | das Kaninchen |
| der Apfel | der Bleistift | das Auto |
| der Kugelschreiber | die Gabel | das Buch |
| der Tisch | der Hund | der Brief |
| die Briefmarke | das Lineal | die Banane |
| die Tochter | das Fenster | die Tür |
| die Schule | der Vater | das Heft |
| die Wand | die Lampe | das Hemd |
| der Polizist | der Vorhang | der Wegweiser |
| das Mädchen | das Blatt | der Bruder |
| der Umschlag | der Schuh | die Autobahn |
| die Uhr | die Krawatte | das Bild |
| das Bad | die Hand | der Finger |
| der Arm | das Bein | der Kopf |
| das Geschenk | der Schrank | die Karte |
| die Mutter | das Bonbon | der Sack |
| der Fuß | der Platz | |

Prepositions are very important in German, because the words which follow them have to change.

You say *mit <u>dem</u> Auto*, but *mit <u>der</u> U-Bahn*;

You say *für <u>meinen</u> Bruder*, but *für <u>meine</u> Schwester*.

It sounds very complicated, but it isn't really. Here are some rules to help you.

## 1 aus, außer, bei, mit, nach, seit, von, zu, gegenüber

| | | | |
|---|---|---|---|
| aus | *out of* | seit | *since* |
| außer | *apart from, besides* | von | *from, of* |
| bei | *at (the house of)* | zu | *to* |
| mit | *with* | gegenüber | *opposite* |
| nach | *after* | | |

These prepositions are always followed by a word ending in 'm', 'r' or 'm'.

Just check the gender of the noun: is it *der, die* or *das*? Then remember:

| | **der** | **die** | **das** |
|---|---|---|---|
| | ⇩ | ⇩ | ⇩ |
| | m | r | m |
| e.g. | dem | der | dem |
| | meinem | meiner | meinem |

## Examples

der Wagen ⇨ mit dem Wagen

die Schule ⇨ nach der Schule

das Fenster ⇨ aus dem Fenster

Try and write these in German:

**a** with my brother _____

**b** after the film _____

**c** at my sister's _____

**d** the girl's bike (the bike of the girl) _____

Did you get them right? You do them like this:

**a** *mit + der Bruder*, so the word following *mit* ends with 'm': *mit meinem Brude*

**b** *nach + der* Film, so the word following *nach* ends with 'm': *nach dem Film*

**c** *bei + die Schwester*, so the word following *bei* ends with 'r ': *bei meiner Schwester*

**d** *von + das Mädchen*, so the word following *von* ends with 'm': *das Fahrrad von dem Mädchen.*

Now try exercise 1 on page 97.

## 2 durch, für, entlang, gegen, ohne, um

| durch | *through* | gegen | *against, towards* |
|-------|-----------|-------|--------------------|
| für | *for* | ohne | *without* |
| entlang | *along* | um | *around* |

These prepositions are always followed by *den, die* or *das* or *einen, eine* or *ein.**

(*Notice there is no 's' here.)

So again, just check the gender of the noun: is it *der, die* or *das*? Then
remember:

|  | **der** | **die** | **das** | |
|------|------|------|------|------|
|  | ⇩ | ⇩ | ⇩ | |
|  | n | e | s | (but NO 's' with *ein, mein,*etc.) |
| e.g. | den | die | das | |
|  | einen | eine | ein | |

## Examples

der Bruder ⇨ für meinen Bruder

die Stadt ⇨ um die Stadt

das Wasser ⇨ durch das Wasser

Try and write these in German:

**a** for my brother _____

**b** without his jacket _____

**c** through the window _____

**d** for a year _____

These work out like this:

**a** *für + der Bruder*, so the word following *für* ends with 'n': *für meinen Bruder*

**b** *ohne + die Jacke*, so the word following *ohne* ends with 'e': *ohne seine Jacke*

**c** *durch + das Fenster*, so the word following *durch* ends with 's': *durch das Fenster*

**d** *für + das Jahr*. The word following *für* normally ends with 's', but we are using *ein*, which cannot end with 's', so it's: *für ein Jahr*.

Now try exercise 2 on page 97.

## 3 an, auf, hinter, in, neben, über, unter, vor, zwischen

| | | | |
|---|---|---|---|
| an | *on (a vertical surface)* | über | *over, above* |
| auf | *on (a horizontal surface)* | unter | *under* |
| hinter | *behind* | vor | *in front of (outside)* |
| in | *in* | zwischen | *between* |
| neben | *next to* | | |

These prepositions work in two ways:

**A** If they are saying **where** something is, they work like group 1,

e.g.  The book is on the table.          *Das Buch ist **auf dem** Tisch.*
     The garage is behind the house.          *Die Garage ist **hinter dem** Haus.*

**B** If they indicate **movement towards** the thing being spoken about, they work like group 2,

e.g.  I drive the car into the garage.    *Ich fahre das Auto* in die Garage.
I am going to the cinema.    *Ich gehe* ins *(in das)* Kino.

Which group do these sentences belong to?

**a** The cat is under the table.

**b** I put it into my pocket.

**c** The library is next to the town hall.

**d** I am going into town.

**e** I'll meet you outside the cinema.

Did you get them right?

**a** Group 1    **b** Group 2    **c** Group 1    **d** Group 2    **e** Group 1

Now try to put the sentences into German.

**a** Die Katze ist unter dem Tisch.

**b** Ich stecke es in meine Tasche.

**c** Die Bibliothek ist neben dem Rathaus.

**d** Ich fahre in die Stadt.

**e** Ich treffe dich vor dem Kino.

Now try exercise 3 on page 98.

When you can get the singular right almost every time, ask your teacher to explain the plural to you.

## 4 Plurals

In the plural, you do not have to worry about the gender of the noun.

**A** The words in **Group 1** are simply followed by a word ending in 'n', e.g. *mit meinen Schwestern*.

Notice also that you put an 'n' on the end of the noun if it does not already have one, e.g. *mit den Fahrrädern*.

Look at the section on plurals (page 90) to help you with plural forms.

**B** The words in **Group 2** are followed by a word ending in 'e', e.g. *für meine Eltern*.

**C** The words in **Group 3** still work in the same way:

Like Group 1 when there is no movement, e.g. *Die Garagen sind hinter* **den Häusern.**

Like Group 2 for **movement towards** the object, e.g. *Wir fahren die Autos in* **die Garagen.**

## Activities

### 1

**a** Ich fahre mit _____ Straßenbahn.

**b** Nach _____ Abendessen mache ich die Hausaufgaben.

**c** Ich wohne in Hamburg seit _____ Jahr.

**d** Ich verbringe den Sommer bei _____ Tante in Berlin.

**e** Das ist ein Geschenk von _____ Oma.

**f** Das Rathaus ist _____ Bahnhof gegenüber.

**g** Ich gehe zu Fuß _____ Schule.

**h** Er ist ein Freund von _____ Schwester.

**i** Ich fahre sehr oft mit _____ Rad.

**j** Fahren Sie _____ Stadion?

### 2

**a** Diese Blumen sind für _____ Mutter.

**b** Gehen Sie hier _____ Straße entlang.

**c** Das kannst du ohne _____ Hilfe machen.

**d** Um _____ Dom gibt es viele schöne Geschäfte.

**e** Vielen Dank für _____ Brief.

**f** Die Familie sitzt um _____ Tisch.

**g** Ich habe es für _____ Bruder gekauft.

**h**  Ohne _____ Partner kann ich nicht Tennis spielen.

**i**  Wir machen einen Spaziergang _____ Fluß entlang.

**j**  Er warf den Ball durch _____ Fenster.

**3**

**a**  In _____ Schlafzimmer gibt es ein Bett.

**b**  Meine Schuhe sind unter _____ Bett.

**c**  Der Tisch ist in ___ Mitte des Zimmers.

**d**  Ich habe viele Poster an _____ Wand.

**e**  Der Stuhl ist neben _____ Tisch.

**f**  Ich hänge meine Kleider in _____ Schrank.

**g**  Meine Jacke hängt hinter _____ Tür.

**h**  Um zehn Uhr gehe ich in _____ Bett.

**i**  Mein Bruder darf nicht in _____ Zimmer kommen.

**j**  Das Badezimmer ist neben _____ Schlafzimmer.

**4**

*This exercise combines all the prepositions.  See how much you have learned!*

**a**  Ich gehe mit _____ Mutter einkaufen.

**b**  In _____ Fußgängerzone kann man sehr gut einkaufen.

**c**  Nach _____ Schule mache ich die Hausaufgaben.

**d**  Mit _____ Taschengeld kaufe ich Bonbons und CDs.

**e**  Der Bleistift?  Er liegt auf _____ Tisch.

**f**  Kannst du das alles in _____ Küche bringen?

**g**  Das Auto ist in _____ Garage.

**h**  Ich fahre mit _____ Bus _____ Schule.

**i**  Ich bin mit _____ Freund in _____ Kino gegangen.

**j**  Wir treffen uns vor _____ Bahnhof und dann gehen wir in _____ Café.

For the reading and listening tests it is very important that you learn the question words well. Many candidates give the wrong answer because they do not read the question words carefully enough.

| | |
|---|---|
| wer | *who* |
| was | *what* |
| wo | *where* |
| warum | *why* |
| wann | *when* |

*Wer* works like *der.* So:

| | |
|---|---|
| für wen | *for whom (who for)* |
| mit wem | *with whom (who with)* |
| bei wem | *at whose house* |
| von wem | *from whom* |
| wessen | *whose* |

Also useful are:

| | |
|---|---|
| wohin | *where to* |
| wie oft | *how often* |
| welche | *which* |
| wie | *how* |
| wie lange | *how long* |
| was für | *what kind of* |
| wie viel | *how much* |
| wie viele | *how many* |
| bis wann | *until when* |

## 1 Self, Family & Friends

1 **a** Onkel; **b** Haustier; **c** hässlich;
**d** Tante; **e** Sohn

2 der Großvater - die Großmutter;
der Bruder - die Schwester; der Onkel
- die Tante; der Sohn - die Tochter;
der Vetter (*or* der Cousin) - die Kusine

3 **a** Vater   Mutter   Sohn   Vetter
Tochter   Onkel   Kusine   Großvater

**b** Katze   Wellensittich   Vogel
Kaninchen   Hamster   Pferd   Hund
Maus

4 **a** Haar; **b** Freund; **c** Geburtstag;
**d** Taschengeld; **e** Erwachsene

5 alt - jung;   dick - schlank;
schwach – stark;   schön - hässlich;
lang - kurz;   hell - dunkel

6 **1** Oma; **2** Opa; **3** Onkel;
**4** Mutter; **5** Tante; **6** Sohn;
**7** Tochter

7 **Körper:** Schnurrbart, Glatze, Auge,
Haar, Nase

**Haustier:** Kaninchen, Hund,
Meerschweinchen, Katze,
Wellensittich

**Familie:** Vetter, Geschwister,
Zwilling, Erwachsene, Großeltern

8 mittelgroß; buchstabieren; Geburt;
Schnurrbart; verheiratet

## 2 Local Area & Weather

1 **a** sonnig; **b** schneien (es schneit);
**c** heiß; **d** wolkig *or* bewölkt;
**e** regnerisch *or* es regnet;
**f** windig; **g** kalt; **h** neblig

2 **a** der Bahnhof; **b** die Brücke;
**c** die Kirche; **d** das Krankenhaus;
**e** der Zoo; **f** der Marktplatz;
**g** das Denkmal; **h** das Kino

3 **a** der Fluss; **b** die Kirche;
**c** die Kuh; **d** das Dorf;
**e** der Hügel; **f** die Sonne;
**g** das Schaf

4 **Stadt:** Dom; Fußgängerzone;
Vorort; Krankenhaus; Theater

**Land:** Dorf; Hügel; Fluss; Schaf; Feld

**Wetter:** Schauer; neblig; Gewitter;
Donner; Blitz

5 Jugendklub; Sonnenschein;
Krankenhaus; Einkaufszentrum;
Wetterbericht; Schwimmbad;
Höchsttemperatur; Spielplatz

6 heiß - kalt;   kühl - warm;
nass - trocken;   regnerisch -
sonnig;   bewölkt - wolkenlos.

7 **a** die Fußgängerzone;
**b** der Spielplatz; **c** der Zoo;
**d** das Stadion; **e** das Freibad;
**f** das Theater; **g** der Jugendklub

8 **a** Fluss; **b** Einwohner;
**c** hitzefrei; **d** Feld; **e** Vorort *or*
Dorf; **f** Kino; **g** Schnee; **h** Nähe

## 3 School Life

**1 Fächer:** Erdkunde, Geschichte, Kunst, Werken, Informatik, Turnen

**Sachen:** Buch, Heft, Bleistift, Ordner, Lineal

**Zimmer:** Labor, Turnhalle, Aula, Klassenzimmer, Bibliothek

**Personen:** Schüler, Schuldirektor, Lehrer, Partner

**2 a** Erdkunde; **b** Religion;
**c** Biologie; **d** Geschichte;
**e** Mathe *or* Mathematik; **f** Chemie;
**g** Kunst; **h** Französisch

**3 a** Schüler; **b** Physik, Chemie, Biologie (*any order*); **c** Ferien;
**d** Hausaufgaben *or* Schularbeiten;
**e** Grundschule; **f** Kantine;
**g** Orchester; **h** Tafel

**4 a** der Bleistift; **b** das Heft;
**c** der Kugelschreiber (der Kuli);
**d** das Wörterbuch; **e** der Füller;
**f** das Buch; **g** das Lineal;
**h** das Papier.

**5** Informatik - der Computer;
das Labor – Chemie;
die Bibliothek - das Buch;
die Frage - die Antwort;
das Wörterbuch – Französisch;
Mathematik - das Lineal;
Musik - der Chor

**6 a** der Austausch;
**b** der Stundenplan;
**c** die Turnhalle; **d** das Zeugnis;
**e** die Klassenfahrt;
**f** die Hausaufgaben/die Schularbeiten

**7** Kassettenrekorder; Kugelschreiber; Klassenfahrt; Stundenplan; Kindergarten; Wörterbuch; Schuldirektor; Mittagspause; Turnhalle; Hausaufgaben

## 4 The Future: Education & Work

### Education

**1** die Schule, die Oberstufe, das Abitur, bestehen, studieren, das Stellenangebot, der Beruf

**2** die Mittlere Reife   das Abitur
das Resultat   durchfallen
bestehen studieren   der Erfolg

**3** Lebenslauf, Leistung, Lehre;
Stellenangebot, studieren, Student;
Abitur, Arzt, Ausbildung;
Handel, Hochschule, heiraten

**4 a** Tierarzt; **b** Zukunft;
**c** Lehrling; **d** Ingenieur;
**e** Ausbildung; **f** studieren

### Work

**1 a** der Briefträger; **b** der Bäcker;
**c** der Metzger *or* der Fleischer;
**d** der Kassierer; **e** der Mechaniker;
**f** der Zahnarzt; **g** die Sekretärin;
**h** der Polizist

**2 a** der Babysitter; **b** der Mechaniker;
**c** die Stewardess;
**d** der Krankenpfleger *or* die Krankenschwester; **e** der Briefträger;
**f** der Kassierer; **g** die Hausfrau;
**h** der Beamte

3 **a** der Kassierer; der Kaufmann;
der Krankenpfleger *or* die Krankenschwester **b** die Fabrik, die Firma,
das Büro **c** der Bäcker, der
Briefträger, der Babysitter, der Beamte

4 arbeitslos, Arbeitspraktikum,
Briefträger, fotokopieren, Hausfrau,
Kaufmann, Krankenpfleger,
Teilzeitjob

## 5  Travel & Transport

1 Busbahnhof;  Hauptbahnhof;
Bushaltestelle;  Rückfahrkarte;
Hauptverkehrszeit;  Autobahnkreuz;
Inter-City-Zug;  Nahverkehrszug

2 **Auto:**  der Kofferraum;
die Einfahrt;  die Tankstelle;
der Stau;  überholen

**Zug:**  der Bahnsteig;
der Hauptbahnhof;  der Wartesaal;
der Schaffner;  der Zuschlag

**Flugzeug:** der Flughafen;
fliegen;  starten;  landen;  der Flug

3 **a** das Motorrad;  **b** das Auto *or*
der Wagen;  **c** der Bus;
**d** das Mofa;  **e** das Fahrrad;
**f** das Flugzeug;  **g** der Zug;
**h** der Lastwagen

4 einsteigen;  abfahren;  fahren;
überholen;  ankommen;  anhalten;
aussteigen;  zurückkommen

5 **a** Haltestelle;  Tankstelle
**b** Straßenbahn;  Autobahn;
S-Bahn
**c** Abfahrt;  Ausfahrt;  Einfahrt;
Heimfahrt

6 **a** Notausgang;  **b** Lastwagen;
**c** Rückfahrkarte;  **d** Busbahnhof;
**e** Eilzug, Personenzug, D-Zug,
Inter-City-Zug;  **f** Motorrad, Fahrrad;
**g** Reisebus;  **h** Flughafen

7 **a** Verspätung;  **b** Wartesaal;
**c** Führerschein;  **d** Kofferraum;
**e** Parkplatz;  **f** Stau;
**g** Flughafen;  **h** zu Fuß

8 Reifen, Reiseziel *or* Reisepass,
Reisende;
Starten *or* Station, Straßenbahn, Stau;
Fahrer, Fahrplan, Fahrkarte;
Flug, fliegen, Flugzeug

## 6  Holidays, Tourism & Tourist Information

1 **a** die Rundfahrt;  **b** der Prospekt;
**c** das Meer;  **d** buchen;
**e** das Verkehrsamt;  **f** der Urlaub

2 **Landschaft:** der Berg,  der See,
der Strand,  die Insel,  die Küste

**Tour:** besichtigen,  der Reiseführer,
die Stadtrundfahrt,
die Sehenswürdigkeit,  der Turm

**Personen:** der Reiseleiter,
der Zollbeamte,  der Tourist,
der Fremde,  der Gast

3 a Blick; b Strand; c sonnen uns;
d Sonnenbrille; e Sonnencreme;
f Balkon; g Ausflüge;
h Reiseleiter; i gebucht;
j Prospekt

4 a 4; b 5; c 3; d 1; e 2

5 a der Berg; b der Balkon;
c der Strand; d die See or das Meer;
e die Sonnenbrille;
f die Sonnencreme; g das Boot;
h der Turm; i der Reiseleiter

## 7 Accommodation

1 a die Zahnbürste; b die Zahnpasta;
c die Dusche; d der Schlüssel;
e das Zelt; f das Badetuch;
g der Schlafsack; h die Seife

2 a H; b C; c B; d H; e H;
f B; g B; h C; i H;
j C; k H

3 a der Aufzug; der Fahrstuhl;
der Lift

b das Doppelzimmer;
das Einzelzimmer;
das Familienzimmer;
Fremdenzimmer

4 Rasierapparat Waschbecken
Fahrstuhl Handtuch
Jugendherberge Unterkunft
Vollpension Zeltplatz

5 Schlafsack or Speisesaal;
Schlüssel; Seife
Rechnung; Reservierung;
Rasierapparat

6 a Wir übernachten in der
Jugendherberge./ Wir zelten auf dem
Campingplatz.

b Wir bekommen Halbpension:
Frühstück und Abendessen./Wir
bekommen Vollpension: Frühstück,
Mittagessen und Abendessen.

c Wir essen in dem Speisesaal im
Hotel.

d Mein Bruder und ich schlafen in
einem Doppelzimmer.

## 8 People & Places

1 a England; b Frankreich;
c Griechenland; d Amerika;
e Italien; f Belgien;
g Schottland; h Österreich;
i Spanien; j Deutschland

2 England - englisch - der Engländer
Deutschland - deutsch - der Deutsche
Frankreich - französisch - der
Franzose
Italien - italienisch - der Italiener
Griechenland - griechisch - der
Grieche
Spanien - spanisch - der Spanier
die Türkei - türkisch - der Türke
die Schweiz - schweizerisch - der
Schweizer

3 a Englisch; b Französisch;
c Deutsch; d Italienisch;
e Spanisch; f Griechisch;
g Türkisch; h Portugiesisch

4 a die Ostsee; b die Nordsee;
c Köln; d München; e Bayern;
f die Alpen; g der Rhein;
h Berlin

5  a  die Ostsee;  b  die Nordsee;
   c  der Kanal;  d  Wien;
   e  das Mittelmeer;  f  die Schweiz;
   g  die Alpen

6  a  Großbritannien;  b  Frankreich;
   c  Spanien;  d  Deutschland;
   e  Österreich;  f  Belgien;
   g  die Schweiz;  h  Italien

7  a  Italien;  b  Frankreich;
   c  England or Großbritannien;
   d  Amerika;  e  Deutschland

8  a  Brieffreund;  b  die Donau;
   c  Italienisch;  d  die Nordsee;
   e  Bayern;  f  Franzose;
   g  das Mittelmeer;  h  Europa

## 9  Services & Finding the Way

### Services

1  a  die Briefmarke;  b  Vorname;
   c  Familienname;  d  die Straße;
   e  die Hausnummer;
   f  der Umschlag;  g  die Postleitzahl;
   h  die Stadt

2  a  die Briefmarke;
   b  die Postkarte;
   c  der Briefkasten;
   d  die Vorwahlnummer;
   e  die Münze

3  a  wechseln;  b  schicken;
   c  mailen;  d  wählen

4  Making a telephone call.

   den Hörer abnehmen;
   Geld einwerfen;  wählen;
   verbinden;  sprechen;
   auf Wiederhören sagen;
   den Hörer auflegen.

5  a  Brief;  b  schicken;
   c  Postkarte;  d  Telefonzelle;
   e  Telefonkarte

### Finding the Way

1  a  geradeaus;  b  links;  c  rechts;
   d  die Ampel;  e  die Kreuzung;
   f  die Ecke;  g  der Wegweiser;
   h  das Schild

2  hinauf - hinunter;  links - rechts;
   erste - letzte;  suchen - finden

3  a  Entschuldigung!;  b  suche;
   c  Wo;  d  Stadtplan;  e  finden;
   f  gehen;  g  geradeaus;
   h  Nehmen;  i  erste;  j  links;
   k  rechten;  l  ungefähr

4  a  Kreuzung;  b  Stadtplan;
   c  überqueren;  d  Einbahnstraße;
   e  geradeaus;  f  Landkarte;
   g  Richtung

## 10  Accidents, Injuries & Illness

1  a  der Kopf;  b  das Gesicht;
   c  der Hals;  d  die Schulter;
   e  die Brust;  f  der Arm;
   g  der Bauch;  h  die Hand;
   i  der Finger;  j  das Bein;
   k  das Knie;  l  der Fuß

2 **a** das Haar; **b** das Ohr;
   **c** das Auge; **d** die Nase;
   **e** der Schnurrbart; **f** der Mund;
   **g** der Zahn (die Zähne);
   **h** die Zunge

3 **a** G; **b** V; **c** K; **d** V; **e** G;
   **f** G; **g** K; **h** V; **i** G

4 **a** Fieber; **b** verboten;
   **c** Tablette; **d** gesund

5 **a** die Hand; **b** die Stimme;
   **c** der Fuß *or* das Bein; **d** das Ohr;
   **e** der Sonnenbrand;
   **f** die Magenschmerzen;
   **g** die Ohrenschmerzen

6 **a** Ich habe mich erkältet.
   **b** Was ist los?
   **c** Vorsicht!
   **d** Ich habe Fieber.
   **e** Mir ist übel.

7 **a** die Hand, der Finger, der Arm, die
   Pastille

8 das Blut, der Mund, die Brust, die
   Lippe, die Schulter, die Zunge, das
   Knie, das Ohr

## 11   House & Home

1 **a** das Bad  **b** der Tisch
   **c** die Spülmaschine; der
   Kühlschrank; die Waschmaschine;
   der Herd  **d** das Auto
   **e** das Bett; der Kleiderschrank
   **f** das Sofa; der Sessel; der
   Fernseher

2 **a** die Lampe; **b** der Fernseher;
   **c** der Tisch; **d** der Stuhl;
   **e** das Sofa; **f** der Teppich;
   **g** die Blume; **h** das Radio;
   **i** das Telefon; **j** die Tür

3 **a** der Wohnblock;
   **b** das Einfamilienhaus;
   **c** das Reihenhaus;
   **d** das Doppelhaus;
   **e** der Bungalow;
   **f** die Wohnung

4 **a** Doppelhaus, Einfamilienhaus,
   Reihenhaus

   **b** Badezimmer, Esszimmer,
   Schlafzimmer, Wohnzimmer

   **c** Waschmaschine, Spülmaschine

   **d** Kühlschrank; Kleiderschrank

5 **a** clothes; der Kleiderschrank,
   wardrobe

   **b** machine; die Waschmaschine,
   washing machine / die
   Spülmaschine, dishwasher

   **c** house; das Doppelhaus, semi-
   detached / das Einfamilienhaus,
   detached / das Reihenhaus, terraced

   **d** room; das Badezimmer,
   bathroom / das Esszimmer, dining
   room / das Schlafzimmer, bedroom /
   das Wohnzimmer, living room

   **e** roof; der Dachboden, attic

6 **a** der Wecker; **b** der Spiegel;
   **c** die Treppe; **d** die Garage;
   **e** die Blume *or* die Pflanze;
   **f** der Keller; **g** die Möbel;
   **h** der Vorhang

**7 a** O; **b** U; **c** D; **d** O; **e** U;
**f** D; **g** B; **h** O; **i** B

**8** das Dach; der Dachboden;
das Schlafzimmer; die Treppe;
der Flur; der Keller

## 12 Life at Home

**1 a** aufwachen; **b** aufstehen;
**c** essen; **d** trinken;
**e** sich waschen; **f** duschen;
**g** schlafen; **h** kochen

**2** e – d – h – a – g – b – c – f

**3 a** ich dusche; ich wasche mich;
ich putze mir die Zähne

**b** ich wache auf; ich stehe auf; ich
schlafe; der Wecker klingelt

**c** ich koche; ich esse; ich trinke

**4** abräumen N, kochen V, abwaschen N,
decken V, abspülen N, essen B,
plaudern B, vorbereiten V,
abtrocknen N

## 13 Special Occasions

**1 a** der Geburtstag; **b** Weihnachten;
**c** Ostern; **d** Neujahr;
**e** Fasching; **f** Prost or zum Wohl;
**g** das Geschenk; **h** die Einladung

**2 a** Gute; **b** Weihnachten; **c** Wohl

**3** e – c – g – b – a – f – d

**4 a** Weihnachten; **b** Pfingsten;
**c** Namenstag; **d** Karneval

**5** Neujahr - Fasching - Ostern -
Pfingsten - Weihnachten - Silvester

## 14 Healthy Living

**1 a** F; **b** U; **c** F; **d** F; **e** F;
**f** F; **g** U; **h** U

**2 a** sich trimmen; **b** abnehmen;
**c** ungesund; **d** Werbung;
**e** Vegetarier; **f** Sportplatz

**3 a** Tabak/Rauchen; **b** Vegetarier;
**c** Sportplatz; **d** mich trimmen;
**e** Fitnesszentrum; **f** Vitamine;
**g** ungesund; **h** aufgegeben

## 15 Food & Drink

**1 Gemüse:** Erbse, Karotte, Kartoffel,
Kohl, Zwiebel

**Getränke:** Kaffee, Kakao,
Orangensaft, Wasser, Wein

**Obst:** Himbeere, Kirsche, Pflaume,
Weintraube, Zitrone

**2 a** Apfel, Apfelsine, Pfirsich, Himbeere,
Banane, Zitrone, Erdbeere, Birne

**b** Bier, Wein, Kakao, Sprudel, Tee,
Cola, Wasser, Kaffee

**3** Aprikose, Apfel, Apfelsine
Spiegelei, Spaghetti, Sprudel
Kalbfleisch, Kartoffel, Karotte
Schinken, Schokolade, Scheibe

**4** die Kartoffel; der Schinken;
die Birne; der Reis; der Kohl;
der Pfeffer; das Salz; das Obst;
der Käse; die Wurst

**5 a** die Banane, die Zitrone

**b** die Bockwurst, die Bratwurst, die Currywurst

**c** Erdbeere, Himbeere, Vanille, Zitrone

**d** das Kalbfleisch, das Rindfleisch, das Schweinefleisch, der Schinken, das Steak

**e** die Butter, der Joghurt, die Margarine, die Milch, der Käse, die Sahne

**6 a** Brot mit Butter;
**b** Fisch mit Pommes frites;
**c** Salz und Essig *or* Pfeffer;
**d** Erdbeeren mit Sahne;
**e** Milch und Zucker

**7 a** der Apfel; **b** die Erbse;
**c** die Zitrone; **d** die Zwiebel;
**e** der Schinken; **f** der Tee;
**g** die Chips

**8 a** der Apfel; **b** der Kaffee;
**c** der Käse; **d** der Keks;
**e** der Reis; **f** der Senf;
**g** der Tee; **h** die Kartoffel

## 16 Eating Out

**1 a** die Gabel; **b** der Löffel;
**c** das Messer; **d** das Glas;
**e** der Kellner; **f** der Topf;
**g** die Tasse; **h** die Serviette

**2** Braten - Fleisch, roast - meat;
Getränk - Bier, drink - beer;
Kännchen - Kaffee, pot - coffee;
Kellner - Trinkgeld, waiter - tip;

Nachtisch - Eis, sweet - ice-cream;
schmecken - lecker, to taste - tasty;
Vorspeise - Suppe, starter - soup

**3** f, g, c, i, h, b, a, d, e

**4** bestellen, bezahlen, Becher
Schale, schmecken, Schnitzel
Menü, Messer, Mehrwertsteuer
Tasse, Topf, Teller

**5** Speisekarte, bestellen, Vorspeise, Hauptgericht, Nachtisch, bezahlen, Trinkgeld

**6 a** das Restaurant, das Café, die Imbissstube

**b** der Becher, die Tasse, das Glas

**c** die Vorspeise, das Hauptgericht, der Nachtisch

**7 a** Speisekarte; **b** probieren;
**c** Getränk; **d** Vorspeise;
**e** Geschmack

## 17 Leisure Activities

**1 a** reiten; **b** fernsehen; **c** segeln;
**d** Ski fahren; **e** lesen; **f** angeln;
**g** tanzen; **h** Rad fahren;
**i** fotografieren; **j** gewinnen

**2** das Schwimmbad - das Hallenbad;
das Hobby - die Freizeit;
üben - trainieren; treffen - ausgehen;
die Gruppe - die Mannschaft

3 **a** der Comic, der Roman, die Zeitung / Zeitschrift

**b** Basketball, Schach, Tischtennis, Volleyball

**c** der Sänger, das Instrument, das Klavier, das Konzert, das Lied

**d** der Eintritt, der Film, der Schauspieler, der Sitz, der Untertitel, die Vorstellung,

4 Angeln: A; Badminton: P; Basketball: M; Fußball: M; Rad fahren: A; Reiten: A; Schach: P; Ski fahren: A; Schwimmen: A; Tanzen: P; Tennis: P; Tischtennis: P; Volleyball: M

5 **a** Theaterstück;
**b** Tischtennis;
**c** Fußball, Volleyball, Basketball;
**d** Schlittschuh;
**e** Untertitel;
**f** Schauspieler;
**g** Schwimmbad, Hallenbad, Freibad;
**h** Endspiel, Videospiel.

6 **a** programmiere; **b** sehe;
**c** schwimme; **d** fotografiere;
**e** sammle

7 geschwommen; besucht; gewonnen; getroffen; gelesen

**a** Ich habe meine Oma besucht.

**b** Ich habe im Schwimmbad geschwommen.

**c** Ich habe die Zeitschrift gelesen.

**d** Ich habe meine Freunde getroffen.

**e** Die Mannschaft hat im Endspiel gewonnen.

8 **Lesen:** der Comic, der Krimi, der Roman, die Zeitschrift, die Zeitung

**Musik:** das Klavier, das Konzert, das Lied, der Sänger, der Walkman

**Kino:** der Eintritt, der Horrorfilm, der Schauspieler, der Untertitel, die Vorstellung

## 18 People & Personalities

1 **a** arm; **b** faul; **c** freundlich;
**d** höflich; **e** schüchtern;
**f** traurig; **g** glücklich; **h** böse

2 **a** doof: - ; **b** launisch: - ;
**c** nett: + ; **d** unhöflich: - ;
**e** faul: - ; **f** ungeduldig: - ;
**g** freundlich: + ; **h** brav: +

3 **a** amüsant, interessant

**b** glücklich, freundlich, höflich, ehrlich

**c** lebendig, geschwätzig, fleißig, ruhig, witzig, vorsichtig

4 dumm: intelligent; laut: leise; glücklich: traurig; faul - fleißig; ernst - witzig; optimistisch - pessimistisch; geduldig - ungeduldig; geschwätzig - schüchtern

5 You can check your answers in the list on pages 68-69.

6 **a** böse; **b** faul; **c** schüchtern;
**d** arm; **e** berühmter; **f** ernst;
**g** altmodisch; **h** ehrlich

## 19 Meeting people

**1** letzte Woche; vorgestern; gestern; heute; morgen; übermorgen; nächste Woche; nächstes Jahr

**2 a** Samstag, der elfte Januar
**b** Mittwoch, der zweiundzwanzigste März
**c** Donnerstag, der neunzehnte Mai
**d** Sonntag, der achte Dezember
**e** Freitag, der dreißigste November
**f** Dienstag, der fünfzehnte Oktober
**g** Montag, der vierzehnte Juli
**h** Donnerstag, der zwölfte August

**3 a** eine Minute; **b** ein Jahr;
**c** eine Woche; **d** ein Tag;
**e** das Wochenende; **f** ein Monat

**4 a** A; **b** L; **c** A; **d** L; **e** A;
**f** L; **g** A; **h** A

**5 a** Samstag, Sonnabend
**b** der Morgen, der Vormittag
**c** der Moment, der Augenblick
**d** jetzt, nun
**e** jeden Tag, täglich

**6 a** Donnerstag; **b** Mittwoch;
**c** Sonntag; **d** Freitag

**7 a** manchmal; **b** hoffentlich;
**c** vorhaben; **d** Nachmittag;
**e** Sonnabend

**8 a** Abend, Sonnabend: evening, Saturday;

**b** kommen, mitkommen / willkommen: to come, to come with someone / welcome;

**c** Mittag, Vormittag / Nachmittag: midday, morning / afternoon;

**d** morgen, übermorgen: tomorrow, day after tomorrow;

**e** gestern, vorgestern: yesterday, day before yesterday;

**f** Woche, Wochenende: week, weekend;

**g** finden, stattfinden: to find, to take place;

**h** Punkt, Treffpunkt: point / dot, meeting place.

**9 a** übermorgen (über 'mor' 'gen')

**b** der Nachmittag ('der' nach 'Mittag')

**c** ein langes Wochenende

## 20 Shopping & Money

**1 a** das Bonbon; **b** der Umschlag;
**c** der Korb; **d** die Dose;
**e** die Kreditkarte;
**f** der Scheck; **g** die Kasse;
**h** das Portemonnaie

**2 a** W; **b** M; **c** C; **d** C; **e** M;
**f** C + W; **g** C; **h** C; **i** W;

**3 a** die Bäckerei;
**b** die Schreibwarenhandlung;
**c** die Buchhandlung;
**d** die Konditorei;
**e** die Metzgerei / die Fleischerei;
**f** das Lebensmittelgeschäft;
**g** das Süßwarengeschäft ;
**h** der Tabakladen;
**i** die Apotheke / die Drogerie

4 **a** geöffnet;
**b** Korb / Einkaufswagen;
**c** Auswahl; **d** Flasche; **e** Dose;
**f** Dutzend; **g** Regal; **h** abteilung;
**i** Kilo; **j** Kasse; **k** Quittung;
**l** preiswert; **m** Tasche

5 **a** Tasche, Brieftasche: bag, wallet;
**b** Markt, Supermarkt: market,
supermarket;
**c** Karte, Kreditkarte: ticket / map,
credit card;
**d** Stück, Eurostück: piece, one
euro coin;
**e** kaufen, verkaufen: to buy, to sell;
**f** Fenster, Schaufenster: window,
display window;
**g** Zeit, Geschäftszeit / Öffnungszeit:
time, opening hours;
**h** Haus, Kaufhaus: house,
department store;
**i** Geld, Bargeld: money, cash;
**j** geben, ausgeben: to give, to spend

6 ausverkauft, Buchhandlung,
Lebensmittelgeschäft, Abteilung,
Metzgerei, Einkaufswagen,
Schaufenster, Untergeschoss,
kostenlos

7 **a** der Euro, der Cent

**b** der Euro, der Cent

**c** der Rappen, der Franken

**d** das Bargeld, der Scheck, die
Kreditkarte

**e** die Dose, die Flasche, die Tüte,
(der Karton, die Packung, die
Schachtel, das Päckchen, das Paket)

**f** das Gramm, das Kilo, das Pfund

## 21 Fashion & Clothes

1 **a** der Hut; **b** der Regenschirm;
**c** der Schuh; **d** die Hose;
**e** das Kleid; **f** die Krawatte / der
Schlips; **g** das T-Shirt; **h** der Scha

2 **a** Anzug, Schlafanzug, Badeanzug:
suit, pyjamas, swimming costume

**b** Mantel, Regenmantel: overcoat,
raincoat

**c** Wolle, Baumwolle: wool, cotton

**d** Lippen, Lippenstift: lips, lipstick

**e** Hose, Badehose: trousers,
swimming trunks

**f** Schuh, Handschuh: shoe, glove

**g** Ring, Ohrring: ring, earring

3 **a** der Schlips, die Krawatte

**b** grau, grün, gelb, gold

**c** der Pullover, der Ring, die Shorts,
die Jeans

**d** anziehen, ausziehen, umziehen,
vorziehen

4 **a** der Handschuh; **b** der Hut;
**c** der Ohrring; **d** der Schal;
**e** die Socke / der Schuh;
**f** die Hose

5 **a** anprobieren; **b** Größe;
**c** Badehose; **d** Regenmantel,
Regenschirm; **e** Farbe;
**f** bequem; **g** wasserfest /
wasserdicht

6 Kleidung, Krawatte, Knopf
  Schal, Schlips, schick
  Größe, grün / grau / gold, Gürtel
  Paar, Pullover, Parfum / Pyjama

7 a grün; b gelb; c grau;
  d rot, gelb (orange), grün; e rot;
  f gelb, weiß; g rot, weiß, blau;
  h schwarz, rot, gold;
  i rot, weiß, rot; j weiß

## 22 Current Affairs & Social Issues

1 a der Vandalismus; b die Graffiti;
  c der Alkohol; d der Müll;
  e das Recycling; f die Abgase;
  g die Obdachlosigkeit;
  h die Arbeitslosigkeit; i der Lärm

2 a Abfall, Abfalleimer: rubbish,
  waste paper basket

  b Müll, Mülltonne: rubbish, dustbin

  c Umwelt, Umweltverschmutzung /
  umweltfreundlich: environment,
  pollution / environmentally friendly

  d Flasche, Mehrwegflasche: bottle,
  returnable bottle

  e werfen, wegwerfen: to throw, to
  throw away

  f geben, ausgeben: to give, to spend

3 a Abfalleimer; b schmutzig;
  c sparen; d trennen; e Dieb;
  f aufgeben; g obdachlos;
  h (Mehrweg) flaschen

4 sauber = clean; Dieb = thief;
  Energie = energy; Welt = world;
  Luft = air; aktuell = topical
  Gewalt = violence; Lärm = noise

## Prepositions

1 a der b dem c einem
  d meiner e meiner f dem
  g zur (*zu der* is usually shortened to
  *zur*) h meiner i dem j zum (*zu
  dem* is usually shortened to *zum*)

2 a meine b die c meine
  d den e deinen f den
  g meinen h einen i den j das

3 a dem (or *meinem*) b dem
  c der d der e dem f den
  g der h ins (*in das* is usually
  shortened to *ins*) i mein
  j dem (or *meinem*)

4 a meiner b der c der
  d meinem e dem f die
  g der h dem, zur
  i meinem, das (ins)
  j dem, das (ins)